Conflict and Control in Welfare Policy: The Swedish experience

Arthur Gould

Longman
London and New York

Longman Group UK Limited,
Longman House, Burnt Mill, Harlow,
Essex CM20 2JE, England
and Associated Companies throughout the world.

*Published in the United States of America
by Longman Inc., New York*

First published 1988

British Library Cataloguing in Publication Data
Gould, Arthur
   Conflict and control in welfare policy.
   1. Sweden. Welfare services. Policies
   I. Title
   361′.9485
ISBN 0-582-01381-X

Library of Congress Cataloging in Publication Data
Gould, Arthur.
   Conflict and control in welfare policy.
   p. cm.
   Bibliography: p.
   Includes index.
   ISBN 0-582-01381-X
   1. Public welfare - Sweden. 2. Sweden - Social policy. 3.
Welfare state. I. Title.
HV338.G68 1988
361.6′1′09485-dc19

                                                 88-4560
                                                 CIP

Set in 10/12pt Baskerville Comp/Edit 6400

Produced by Longman Group (FE) Limited
Printed in Hong Kong

Contents

Foreword

Thirty – even twenty – years ago, most social policy research was conducted by teaching academics. In the intervening years specialist research centres and institutes have grown in number, scale and output and the link between teaching and research has seemed a less inevitable one. By the early 1980s that link was being overtly challenged; the Government's drive to reduce public expenditure led it to posit 'teaching only' universities, or departments. Resourcing all universities to undertake research came to be seen as a way of adding to the costs of university education without necessarily adding to its effectiveness.

Arthur Gould's research on social welfare and social control provides an unintended but timely and eloquent re-affirmation of the traditional argument that good teaching and good research go hand in hand. His starting point was a student's need to resolve an intellectual puzzle. In 1983 a newspaper article alleged that disproportionate numbers of children were taken into care in Sweden. The student suggested that this contradicted the idea of Sweden as a model welfare state. Although it might simply be argued that welfare capitalism is riddled with contradictions, of which this is but one, the issue seemed worthy of further consideration.

The student's query provoked lively debate, but it also prompted four years of careful empirical research and a number of study trips to Sweden before the puzzle could be resolved sufficiently to formulate a new body of teaching material. However, what most impressed his colleagues during that time was the determination with which Arthur Gould mastered the Swedish language and immersed himself in Swedish history and culture in order to move beyond stereotypes and beyond the limitations of material in the English language. A small part of Loughborough has, in the process, been transformed into an honorary parish of Swedish society.

The book which has emerged from this research represents an important contribution to social policy and is indicative of the way in which the empirical tradition of social administration has been enriched by the theoretical preoccupations of the past two decades. The late sixties ushered in an era of intellectual excitement in which the old certainties were challenged on all sides. The exploration of welfare activities as mechanisms of social control was a central example of this theoretical and critical realignment. Social policy was stripped of its ideological naïveté and its methodological innocence. But the literature on social control also illustrated the dilemma into which the rush for theory had thrown us all. Social administration was castigated for its earlier addiction to empiricism, yet it had little by way of evidence to offer when it came to testing many of the newer propositions. And the more general the proposition, the more impossible it is to test it within any society.

The relationship between social control and welfare capitalism is certainly one which calls for comparative research. Arthur Gould's response to this challenge was to undertake research comprising four case studies on social control within the Swedish welfare system. The single country study is a vehicle for in-depth qualitative work. It allows close attention to detail and to the nuances of a country's social, economic and political systems. This is what this book provides. It is an example of how another welfare system can be studied not in its totality and in largely descriptive terms, but selectively in order to explore an issue of theoretical significance. The implicit comparison with Britain serves to highlight the significance of cultural differences within the general framework of welfare capitalism. It refines our understanding of social control within and through welfare, and wets the appetite for a larger cross-national study of the same issues. Such an outcome is as good an illustration as any of the continuing case for fostering interaction between teaching and research within higher education.

Adrian Webb
Professor of Social Administration
Loughborough University

Acknowledgements

This book could not have been written without the help and generosity of many people in Sweden, but in particular I would like to thank Åke Svensson, Åsa Lindberg, Haluk Soydan, Leif Holgersson, Lars Grönwall, Sten-Åke Stenberg, Björn Löfholm and Berth Danemark. The Economic and Social Research Council financed the research visit to Stockholm in 1985 which led to Chapter 4 while the Nuffield Foundation enabled me to visit Örebro and Karlskoga for an extended period during 1986 which resulted in the material for the remaining case studies. I am very grateful for their assistance. I would also like to thank my colleagues at Loughborough who have read and criticised my work at various points – Paul Byrne, Janet Ford, Jane Taylor, Ruth Sinclair and Mike Stephens; and lastly, my Swedish teacher, Karin Forsgren-Evans. All quotations from sources in Swedish are my own translations.

We are indebted to the following for permission to reproduce copyright material: the BBC for an extract from *Scandinavian Journey* by J. Hale, BBC Radio 4, 10/8/83; the author, Arthur Gould for an extract from his article 'Social Totalitarianism' from pp 29–39 *Policy and Politics* Vol 15, No 1, 1987

and

Gower Publishing Company Ltd for table 8.1 from p 167 *Limits of The Welfare State* by J. Fry; The Swedish Institute for table 2.3 from pp 3 & 5 *Current Sweden* No's 341 & 295.

We have been unable to trace the copyright holder in table 4.7 from p 88 *Barneverni Nordern* by Turid Vogt Grinde (1985) and would appreciate any information that would enable us to do so.

To Alex, Joe and Toby

PART ONE
The context

CHAPTER ONE

The conflict between welfare and control

INTRODUCTION

It is commonly accepted that many social policies contain elements of social control. It is also commonly accepted that a degree of control is inevitable and desirable. If a young child is cruelly tortured by its parents, then few would doubt the need for the child to be taken into care. For that to happen we would also accept the need for appropriate legislation, a properly financed local authority department, adequately trained social workers and the provision of an institution or a foster home to take care of the child. If a thirteen-year-old girl was discovered to be using hard drugs, we would probably all agree that the authorities and the courts should ensure that the girl's behaviour should be adequately supervised or, again, that she should be removed from her home. We might also accept that a healthy, single, adult male who was well-qualified for a number of jobs that existed in his locality, should not be allowed to claim social assistance indefinitely, and would expect the authorities to take action to prevent him from doing so.[1]

Where cases are as clear cut as the examples above we may say that there is a consensus behind the need for control. But cases are not always clear cut and there is often no such consensus. Instead there are dilemmas and doubts, suspicion and conflict. The conflict might be about the evidence in particular cases, it might be about the way in which the cases are handled by the authorities, it might be about the adequacy of the measures taken, the values or interests on which they are based, or the laws and policies that govern them.

Knowledge of such cases may come to us first hand, through the media or learned publications. On the one hand we may be appalled by the lack of action taken. A child may be beaten to death and we ask what was the family's social worker doing. We read that sexual abuse within families is occurring on a wide scale and wonder why more is not being done. If we know that someone is making multiple claims for social assistance, we want to know why he is not being investigated. Yet we are equally shocked by social workers who appear to 'over-react' to problems and take children from their families unnecessarily, or social security officials who spy on single women claimants who are suspected of living with and being maintained by a man. Whom do we believe when such cases come to light? The clients and claimants, the officials and the social workers, the media or the politicians? What sort of control do we regard as just and necessary? What sort of rules, policies and laws do we regard as appropriate? How do we respond to the demands of this or that pressure group that more or less control is required? On these and other similar issues there is a great deal of debate and conflict in any modern industrial society.

This book is about a conflict that has raged in Swedish welfare policy for the last twenty years about the measures that should be taken to deal with a range of social problems and the extent to which the authorities should be empowered to control people's behaviour, particularly through the administration of social assistance and social services. It is an attempt to examine how a society which has come to be regarded by many as a social democratic paradise, the most successful example of a welfare state functioning within a capitalist economy, has coped with the problem of reconciling the twin demands for welfare and control. But before we enter into that conflict, it would be appropriate to look briefly at how other writers have attempted to explain the existence of and need for social control through welfare in other capitalist societies.

THEORIES OF CONTROL

A consensus view of society would explain the need for control in welfare policy by reference to the need that social systems have for order and stability. It is argued that social systems cannot function without shared norms and values and that it is the job of education and welfare institutions in a complex industrial society to ensure that individuals are adequately socialised and that where socialisation breaks down, the means must exist to maintain an adequate level of conformity, through mechanisms of social control. This would mean that individuals would have to be helped or made to adapt to the needs of society, both in their own interests and in the interests of the wider society. Such an explanation would be adequate to account for the acceptable examples of control that were referred to in the opening paragraph. Through the provision of welfare and control, social services would be seen as strengthening the adaptability and integration of individuals and society. Such a view is rarely held uncritically but it is one that writers such as Richard Titmuss have advocated to a degree.

While there is some justification for seeing the welfare state and social policy in terms of consensus and shared values and interests, such a view has been heavily criticised by many radical writers both in the US and the UK. Piven and Cloward in a study of social assistance in the US qualified the consensus approach by arguing that ruling élites had a much greater impact on the development of social policy than the poorer sections of the population and they acted to protect their own interests not those of the wider society:

> The key to an understanding of relief-giving is in the functions it serves for the larger economic and political order, for relief is a secondary and supportive institution. Historical evidence suggests that relief arrangements are initiated or expanded in the occasional outbreaks of civil disorder produced by mass unemployment, and are then abolished or contracted when political stability is restored. We shall argue that expansive relief policies are designed to mute civil disorder, and restrictive ones to re-inforce work norms.
>
> (Piven and Cloward 1972: p. xiii)

Social control in welfare policy here is regarded as a device whereby powerful groups preserve social stability and reinforce norms and values in order to maintain their own privileges, not the integration and well-being of society as a whole. Moreover, as Handler has argued in a comparison between social work services in the US and the UK, such relief policies, in America, often took the form of social assistance administered by social workers. Since the number of their clients far outweighed the meagre resources at the disposal of social workers, the discretion and control exercised by them were considerable. They could not provide clients with the jobs or the incomes which they required and this inevitably led to methods which emphasised the need for clients to find ways of helping themselves: 'Thus stated this strategy is both rational and humanistic. The problem is that this very simple, decent approach became professionalized; it grew into a manipulative, moralistic attempt at changing behaviour based upon shallow psychological foundations' (Handler 1973: p. xi). This situation, coupled with the trend in the 1970s to move, like Britain, towards integrated, comprehensive departments of social services, led Handler to express concern at the amount of centralised power that was to be exercised over every aspect of clients' social and family lives (Ibid: p. 140). Such power would not be difficult to justify in a country where it had been traditionally thought that there was a 'large, undeserving poor and that welfare should aim at prevention not income maintenance' (Patterson 1986: p. 183).

Similar concerns have been expressed by socialist writers in the UK. The welfare state has been seen, by them, as a product of conflicting class interests. While it may be true, they have argued, that labour movements in capitalist societies have fought for the expansion of welfare expenditure in order to provide health care, education, housing, social security and social services for the working class, the ruling class has only made concessions when it has suited its own interests and purposes. Some social policy measures may have increased the well-being of the working class, it is argued, but others are: '... repressive mechanisms of social control: social work, schools, housing departments, the probation service, social security agencies – all [can be] seen as means of controlling and/or adapting rebellious and non-conformist groups to the needs of capitalism' (Gough 1979: p. 11). Novak described the British social security system as having a 'fixation with the idea that many of those who depend upon it are out to cheat it [which] has given rise to a battery of procedures and investigations' (Novak 1984: p. 42). He compared the 5000 officials appointed to check on social security abuse with the 260 appointed to investigate tax fraud. Although the amount of tax fraud far exceeded social security abuse, investigation of the former resulted in only 184 prosecutions in 1979 compared with 29,000 for the latter (Ibid: p. 44). Golding and Middleton have also described this policy bias as an 'obsession' and one which has found considerable support in the British press. The consequence of newspapers with a mass circulation being almost entirely to the right politically, conducting anti-welfare campaigns, meant that their readers were never given alternative explanations for increases in welfare spending and the decline in their own living standards. As a result, the decision by policy-makers to control and persecute social security claimants, was amplified with considerable media support (Golding and Middleton 1982).

Although British social workers unlike their American and Swedish counterparts do not administer social assistance, most of their clientele come from the deprived sections of society. Their part in the conspiracy to control the poor is also criticised by writers who subscribe to the conflict school of sociological thinking. Kincaid, for example, described them as being: '... indifferent to the broader possibilities of the welfare state and appear content with the limited role they are offered in the present political order' (Kincaid 1975: p. 228). Leonard went further in his introduction to Jones *State social work and the working class* when he described the relationship between the state, social workers and the working class as one 'essentially based on oppression and control' (Jones 1983). Although in a previous text he had implied that radical social workers could exploit the degree of autonomy they had within the ideological state apparatus, he clearly assumed that control was the principal function of social work within a capitalist welfare system (Corrigan and Leonard 1978). Jordan too has described social workers as acting 'uncritically ... as agents of new policies, however restrictive or controlling they may be' (Jordan 1981: p. 145). He attacked the paternalism of the new social services departments for their 'special brand of behavioural manipulation' (Ibid.: p. 147) and their increasing use of control and compulsion in child abuse cases. He further anticipated that conservative governments in the 1980s would put even more emphasis on the control and punishment of clients (Ibid.: p. 150).

As with radical writers in the US, so with British socialist academics, welfare policy is seen as a means of controlling people in order that the interests of capital will be served. Social workers and social security officials, teachers and doctors, may be providers of welfare but they are also agents of a repressive form of social control within capitalist states.

A similar criticism of welfare bureaucrats and professionals is made by writers such as Illich. But whereas the neo-marxists stress the contribution that welfare personnel make to capitalist society as a whole, Illich regards them as being dedicated to the maintenance of their own particular institutions. Educationalists, doctors and social workers seek to make people dependent upon their services. They manipulate them into believing that they cannot learn, solve their own problems or look after their own bodies, without the services of professionals. The welfare professions disable people rather than liberate them. They act in pursuit of their own interests and in order to maintain their institutional empires and meet neither the needs of their clients, nor those of society (Illich 1971, 1976 and 1977). Nor is this view of welfare bureaucrats and professionals shared only by those of a left-wing persuasion. The new right has also been vociferous in claiming that state welfare establishments seek to increase the amount of resources going to them and the size of their respective empires. It is alleged that state welfare monopolies neither reduce inequalities nor solve problems. This new class of welfare practitioners exerts increasing control over policy decisions and at the same time deprives the rest of us of the right to choose or criticise (Anderson *et al* 1981).

So the literature tells us that there are a number of different ways of looking at control through welfare policy. Social control can help individuals and society to adapt to the difficulties and problems they face; it may be the means whereby powerful groups repress and contain deprived, deviant and discontented groups; it may be a form of manipulation by the very administrators and professionals appointed to provide welfare services.

CRITIQUES OF CONSENSUS AND CONFLICT THEORIES

In a review of literature similar to that outlined above, Joan Higgins, has criticised certain deficiencies in theories of control (Higgins 1980). She argues that the link between a ruling capitalist class or 'the system' and welfare policies is plausible but not easy to demonstrate. Such theories rely upon assertion rather than proof. She also suggests that the intention behind policies is assumed from their effects. Thus the fact that the working class has not benefited as much from redistributive policies as was hoped, or that clients have so little influence over the services provided for them may not be because there is some conscious conspiracy by élite groups to achieve such ends. She goes on to say that while some policies and measures are clearly intended to repress or control, there are many aspects of health care, social security, education and housing where it would be very difficult to argue that that there was a controlling intention or effect. Moreover, in another work, she argues that there are many vulnerable groups who benefit from welfare provision who are not in the least bit threatening or disruptive. The motive to help the blind, handicapped and elderly can hardly be to contain and control their rebellious potential (Higgins 1978: pp. 17–18). She concludes her critique of social control theories by making the point that there are many social workers, and by implication, doctors, teachers and administrators, who see their roles in a rather radical way and not as agents of social control. On the contrary they see their task in terms of counteracting inequalities within the system and, together with their clients, attempting to change the structure of society (Higgins 1980: p. 22).

Broadly speaking, Higgins is rather distrustful of attempts to reduce the state, the system or professional groups to monolithic forces that act in a concerted fashion to control, manipulate and repress the recipients of welfare services. This does not mean that she does not value the theories of control that have been put forward, only that they have certain deficiencies which future work should seek to avoid:

> The way forward now seems to be to expand the middle ground between the empiricism of traditional social administration, on the one hand, and abstract theorizing on the other. We can overcome some of the methodological problems of social control theories by testing them more rigorously against empirical data. Similarly the introspection of social administration can be countered if we look to theory for clues about general trends and patterns of change in social policy. It has always been unfashionable to advocate a 'middle-range' approach, presumably on the grounds that middle-range theorists can stand for anything or nothing. However, social control theories of social policy hold out exciting possibilities for the development of critical and insightful theory, and a compromise between theoretical and empirical perspectives must be reached if the best of both approaches is not to be rejected out of hand. (Higgins 1980: p. 23)

Although contributors to *Social control and the state* by Cohen and Scull were primarily concerned with the issues of crime and mental illness rather than social welfare, much of what they have had to say reinforces Higgins' argument. Stedman-Jones, Rothman and Ignatieff all found the concept of social control, as used by both functionalists and marxists, far too encompassing. Every agency was an agency of control, every institution a socialising one. The concept was 'flabby' (Cohen and Scull 1985: p. 109). While it was recognised that the earlier naivety of reformist and evolutionary accounts of social control required the corrective of conflict analysis, as Ignatieff pointed out, the functionalism of the 1920s: '. . . placed so much stress on the consensual that it neglected the coercive; [whereas] the social control literature of the 1970s exaggerated the coercive at the expense of the consensual' (Cohen and Scull 1985: p. 99). Ignatieff went on to claim that *'the powers of moral and punitive enforcement are distributed throughout civil society'* (Ibid: p. 100, my italics). In this view he was supported by Mayer who claimed that too often social reforms were dismissed by latter-day historians as examples of social control on the basis of little evidence and with little recognition of the complexity surrounding the emergence and implementation of the reforms. He added: 'Useful analysis requires the ability to distinguish the differences as well as recognise the similarities of various controlling efforts; different types of controlling efforts imply different functional or motivational meanings' (Ibid: p. 25).

This book has been written in the hope that it may contribute something towards the aims set out by Joan Higgins, and take account of some of the reservations made by the contributors to *Social control and the state*. It is important that attempts are made to relate theory more closely to empirical data and there is a need to get away from a blanket assumption that particular systems, classes or professional groups are intent upon social control in some monolithic way.

Neo-marxists go some way to recognising this when they argue, like Ian Gough, that the state in a capitalist society, has *relative autonomy* (Gough 1979: p. 44). By this they mean that the state is a focus for class struggle and that even if the interests of the capitalist class are paramount, other groups and classes may succeed in advancing their interests. Measures of welfare and control will therefore be the result of conflicting class forces. This is qualified even further by the recognition that within any class or group there will be factions that will disagree with each other about the means and the ends of welfare and control policies. Pluralist writers would also accept the need to see the state as a focus for competing interests and would regard classes and political parties as consisting of a number of groups with differing aims and values. Where neo-marxists and pluralists part company is over the emphasis that the former place upon the long-term interests of capitalism. If you assume that all welfare policies ultimately function in the long-term interests of capital, this is bound to make you suspicious of even the most progressive reforms. Be that as it may, for the purposes of this book, the intention has been to get away from any assumption that all examples of social control in welfare policy operate in the conspiratorial interests of any homogeneous party, class or group. The intention has been to explore the dynamics, inconsistencies and conflicts that arise over issues of control.

DIFFERENCES BETWEEN CAPITALIST SOCIETIES

There is one other area in which previous studies have been lacking and which may be rectified somewhat by the present book, and that is in the fact that most of the theories of social control that have been advanced have been rooted empirically in those capitalist societies in which political parties of the right have been dominant. While this may be the norm, there have been some in which socialist parties and labour movements have had a considerable influence. Generalisations about capitalist societies which lump the US, Japan, West Germany, the UK and Sweden together for example, are on tricky ground. It is clear that they are each examples of advanced capitalist economies. And it is also clear that they each have welfare systems which in some ways are the result of working-class struggle and in others satisfy the needs of capital or professional and occupational interests, but beyond that, generalising becomes difficult.

For example, it has been said generally, of all welfare systems, that stigma attaches to the recipients of social assistance (Heidenheimer 1983: p. 204, Wilson 1982: p. 64) but the extent to which a particular system relies upon social assistance varies considerably. More emphasis is placed upon social assistance by the US and the UK compared with West Germany and Sweden, while the latter have a more positive and a more coherent approach to social insurance (Heidenheimer *et al* 1983: pp. 217 and 221). It may therefore follow that one will find less stigma and control in West Germany and Sweden than in the US and the UK.

Moreover while Japan has been almost exclusively conservative throughout its history, and the UK, in spite of brief periods of Labour Government, remains very much a conservative country, Sweden is unique in that, since 1932, the social democratic party, with the exception of the years 1976–82, allied with a powerful trade union movement, has dominated the political scene. While there are some aspects of welfare which may be attributed to the intrinsic characteristics of capitalist society *per se*, Castles has argued that the nature of public welfare is greatly influenced by whether a political system is dominated by parties of the left or right (Castles 1978). Moreover, if this applies to welfare policies as a whole, might it not also apply to the controlling elements of those policies? Yet although much is known about Sweden's reputation as a welfare leader, almost nothing has been published in English about the sorts of conflicts that have arisen there between the twin aims of welfare and control. It is hoped in what follows that something may be added to our more general knowledge of the function of welfare and control within a capitalist system, by concentrating on the controlling aspects of the social welfare policies of a social-democratic state and in particular upon the debate about the use of compulsory measures within Swedish social services.

CONTROL AND WELFARE IN SWEDEN

It will be seen that some of the evidence presented later would seem to lend support to both consensus and conflict theorists. In support of a consensus approach to social control, it may be argued that Sweden is a society in which there is a shared value system. There does indeed seem to be a widespread acceptance of temperance attitudes and policies. The disapproval of alcohol and drug abuse leads directly to the custody of children affected by abuse, the reluctance to hand out social assistance to abusers unconditionally, and the sometimes compulsory supervision, treatment and care of abusers. Indirectly, it might be said, that temperance attitudes are an indication of a wider willingness to intervene in people's private lives for their own good. Such things have often been said about Swedish culture. If this is so, then studies of the relationship between welfare and control, ought to consider the possibility that what at first may appear to be evidence of the controlling impulses of social workers, politicians or a dominant class, might be a reflection of widely held attitudes that cannot simply be explained by or reduced to the interests of specific social groups.

Not that there isn't plenty of evidence for that as well. It will be seen that the most right-wing party in Sweden is the one that most consistently demands controlling measures in welfare policy. But it is also the case that, although parties of the left are divided on the issue, strong socialist factions are also in favour of more controlling measures. Neo-marxist arguments have sometimes dismissed similar examples in other countries as illustrative of the way in which capitalism gains the compliance and co-operation of the leadership of working-class movements. But here, as will be shown in Chapter 2, we are dealing with a socialist party that has established itself as the natural party of government over decades. In the field of welfare it has been able to achieve what no other social democratic or socialist government has been able to achieve. If it has been able to resist the right and the ruling class in creating the enormous edifice of the welfare state, how can it be said that in the tiny area of social welfare it has caved in to reactionary pressures? Moreover, support amongst socialists for control is not confined to the leadership or even to the membership of the SAP (The Social Democratic Workers' Party).

Members of the far left, and equally far removed from the seat of government, have also been active in demanding restrictive welfare policies. A more plausible answer is that many socialists take a hard line on such issues because it suits *their* ends not those of capital or capitalists.

The way they see it, it does not further the interests of the working class, or that of socialism, to encourage the growth of welfare dependency. If necessary, strong and compulsory measures have to be taken to counteract it. This is not caving in to the demands of the propertied class but an insistence that a strong and disciplined labour movement must consist of independent workers. Tough-minded socialists may agree on ends with their more liberally-minded counterparts – a welfare state, full employment, a socialist society – but they do not necessarily agree on the means whereby those ends may be achieved.

It therefore seems reasonable to suggest that future studies of the conflict between welfare and control might consider the possibility that controlling measures advocated by left-wing politicians, left-wing governments and left-wing local authorities might be as much examples of socialist discipline as capitalist repression. There have been many disputes within British social policy where a conflict between libertarian left-wing welfare workers and more tough-minded Labour councillors has been interpreted as a left–right dispute, with the activists able to claim themselves as the true representatives of the working class and their opponents as capitalist lackeys. It might make more sense on such occasions if it was accepted that it was at least possible, both to advocate policies of control and remain socialist. Control then would not automatically be regarded as a capitalist weapon.

This study also gives some support to the argument that welfare bureaucrats and professionals are intent upon forcing the demand for their services upon society at large. Such an interpretation of the behaviour of those employed in various welfare agencies in Sweden, who advocate greater measures of control and compulsion, is certainly possible. But what is to be made of the fact that similar people are opposed at every level of organisation to the retention or extension of control measures? This conflict does not even represent a straight hierarchical split between those in powerful positions and those dealing with clients. The majority of directors of social services in Sweden are on the side of reducing their powers to compulsorily intervene in the lives of people with social problems, as are many social workers. How does this square with the notion that the welfare professions attempt to make people dependent upon their services? There are many who argue exactly the opposite. They say that social assistance should become automatic for some groups so that clients will *not* have to come under the scrutiny of the social services. They say that it is better that clients come to them for support and help on a voluntary basis and that compulsion has no place in welfare. Hardly the best way of forcing your services upon someone!

What this study does overwhelmingly endorse is Higgins' plea for getting away from monolithic, functionalist theories and homogeneous interest groups and classes. If welfare itself can be seen as meeting the requirements of capital, the needs of the working class and the interests of professional groups, surely the same can be said of measures of control. Moreover, if factions within capital can disagree about the extent of and need for control, so can professional groups, socialists and the working class. Control is not just about repression, it is also about acceptable standards of behaviour, order and organisation, discipline and self-reliance. While we may want to create a society in which repression and coercion are reduced to a minimum, we will never create a decent society which can do without moral standards, social order and organisation, nor one in which individuals can dispense with self-discipline and self-reliance.

THE ORIGINS AND PLAN OF THIS BOOK

This study has arisen out of an interest in comparative social welfare. In order to understand how social policy has developed and with what purposes, interests and aims, it is necessary to look at societies other than one's own. The difficulty for anybody faced with a country like Sweden, however, is that a reliance on material published in English, imposes severe limitations on research and is likely to result in a very superficial view of a country's welfare policies. For this reason most of our knowledge of what goes on in that society has been very one-sided. The accepted view of Sweden as a welfare state miracle has been based largely upon the impressive size of the state welfare budget and the scale and quality of its services. It is seen as *the people's home*, founded upon a generous, humane and social-democratic ideal. It is the contention of this study that while this picture is not false, it is far from complete.

The consequence of this incomplete picture is that those who have attempted to make generalisations about the welfare state and social policy in capitalist society, have, when it comes to references to Sweden, had to rely upon a stereotype. As a result, the Swedish model has been used to reinforce existing theories and preconceptions. Fabians and social democrats have focused upon the welfare achievements, neo-marxists have stressed persisting inequalities and conservatives have seized upon any evidence of social or economic malaise – in order to justify whatever view of the welfare state they already had. It is hoped that this study will give some cause for thought before the welfare state gets slotted back into people's mental strait-jackets.

The plan of the book is as follows: Chapter 2 looks at the development of the Swedish welfare state and shows how, in comparison with other countries, it has come to be regarded as a model for social democratic reform. This chapter relies almost exclusively upon material that has been available for some time in English, whereas the rest of the book is based upon material which hitherto has not been translated. Chapter 3 examines an area of Sweden's welfare state which has received very little attention outside Sweden – that of the development of those social services primarily concerned with the poor, the deprived and those with social problems. It shows how the influence of the old poor law and a strong temperance movement upon those services became the focus of a vigorous debate in the 1960s and 1970s which culminated in major legislative reforms in 1982. The debate is evidence of a major conflict between those who argue that the best way to help people with social problems is to rely largely on their self-motivation, and those who say that there must be a greater reliance on compulsory measures, to make people independent of state help.

Part two of the book is concerned with the continuation of that conflict into the 1980s. It is this section which forms the empirical and original basis of the whole study. In each of the four case studies presented there is a core element or issue which is located in a wider context. Chapter 4 investigates the allegation that too many children are taken into care in Sweden, by comparing the official statistics of the UK and the Scandinavian countries. It concludes with a description of the debate between various pressure groups and individuals about the appropriateness of existing methods for dealing with problem families, the justification for state intervention, and the possible link between children in care and the problems of alcohol and drug abuse. Chapter 5 describes the methods Swedish social welfare committees have used in the past and more recently, for supervising and helping families and children with problems. Prior to the reforms of 1982, such measures contained a strong element of compulsion and control; after 1982, they were mainly voluntary. The results of a survey carried out in two local authorities illustrate the dilemmas faced by a policy designed to replace control measures with measures of voluntary support. Chapter 6 is concerned with the provision of social assistance, which in Sweden, remains the responsibility of local authorities and social workers. It explores the conflict between those who see social assistance as a right and those who see it as conditional upon recipients making an attempt to help themselves, principally through the controversy surrounding the methods used by a group of social workers in Stockholm. Chapter 7 is concerned with the problems of alcoholics and drug addicts and the extent to which help and treatment for such people should rely more on a voluntary or a compulsory approach. Comparisons with the scale of similar problems faced in other countries are made; the positions taken by influential pressure groups are outlined; and the forceful policy advocated by one local authority is described. The possibility that more controlling legislation may soon be re-introduced, in the light of the AIDS problem, is also mentioned.

Part three is concerned with attempts to explain the controlling elements in Swedish welfare policy and begins in Chapter 8, with an examination of the merits and deficiencies of four different critiques. In Chapter 9 a framework incorporating concepts of inequality and control is developed and applied to an analysis of the case studies. It concludes with the suggestion that a combination of marxist and Durkheimian approaches offers a fruitful way towards a more general theory of the relationship between welfare policy and social control. In the last chapter it is argued that social control in a genuine welfare state must not be confused with the repressive control that characterises other welfare systems.

NOTE

1. I have used the term social assistance throughout the book to refer to those means-tested cash benefits which exist in most welfare systems to help those in need, who have no other source of income or social insurance entitlement, on which to depend for their daily living needs. In the UK this is referred to as Supplementary Benefit. Public assistance and Livelihood Assistance are two terms used in other countries. In Sweden the old term, prior to 1982 was Socialhjälp, the new one is Socialbidrag. Both can be loosely translated as social assistance.

CHAPTER TWO

The Swedish welfare state

INTRODUCTION

The aim of this chapter is to show why it is that Sweden is believed to be *the* welfare state. It will be seen that the evidence is strong, though not conclusive by any means. In the space of one chapter it is not possible to paint a totally accurate picture of Swedish welfare, and the data and examples given are merely intended to represent some of the salient features that have led to this belief. It will be clear later, from Chapter 8, that there are also many people who have dissented from this view. It is however, necessary to present the stereotype, if only to enable the reader to make sense of later qualifications and reservations, and to be aware that when we come to discuss aspects of control, we are talking about a capitalist society in which social democracy has achieved a great deal. What follows is a brief outline of the country, its labour movement and the main features of its welfare state. This leads to an account of some comparative statistics and to the favourable comments made by many writers when they have attempted to compare Sweden with other countries. The chapter concludes with a summary of the important economic and political changes that have taken place since the mid-1970s.

THE COUNTRY AND ITS REPUTATION

Although twice the geographical size of Great Britain, Sweden has a population of only 8.3 million people, compared with our 55 million. Its early economic development was based very much upon

17

the raw materials of iron ore and timber, but it has since become widely known for the quality of its engineering and other manufactured products. For a country of so few people, Sweden is the base for an impressive number of internationally renowned private companies, such as Volvo, Electrolux, Saab-Scania, Ericsson and the Nobel Industries. The post-war success of the Swedish economy, the expansion of its welfare state and the high standard of living enjoyed by the mass of the population encouraged many observers to see Sweden as a model of what social democracy could achieve. During the 1960s Sweden came to be seen as a society that had found a successful 'middle way' between the extremes of capitalism and socialism. It was a prototype for others to follow (Tomasson 1970). For many reformists it showed that the power of the people could be expressed through democratic institutions. Violent revolution was not the way to a humane, egalitarian society. Change could be achieved peacefully and gradually. The roots of that change went back to the last century, Sweden's late industrialisation and the growth of its labour movement.

THE LABOUR MOVEMENT

Industrialisation came to Sweden late in the nineteenth century and in common with all other capitalist societies the process was accompanied by a great deal of hardship and poverty. In rapid response three popular movements arose – the labour movement, the temperance movement and the free church movement. Most of their members came from the lower strata of society and it was not uncommon for someone to be a member of all three movements (Lundqvist 1975). The establishment of the Social Democratic Workers' Party (SAP) in 1899, the federation of manual workers' trade unions (LO – Landsorganisation) in 1898, and the Swedish Cooperative Union and Wholesale Society (KS) in 1899 ensured the working class of a high degree of political representation and industrial muscle in the early decades of the century. This development culminated in the first democratically elected (albeit in coalition with the Liberals) socialist government in the world in 1920.

This government was short-lived and not particularly effective but the economic crisis that came at the end of the 1920s resulted in the election of a social democratic government in 1932 that was to enjoy an unbroken period of rule for 44 years. From tentative beginnings the social democrats began to build a 'peoples' home' that was to excite world-wide admiration. Swedish neutrality in two world wars spared the economy from devastation and the Second World War in particular provided Swedish business with the remarkable opportunity to make money out of Britain and Germany. This tremendous boost to the economy was seized on by the social democrats to build a welfare state based upon full employment. Although the SAP had abandoned its early marxist leanings and had set its face against wholesale nationalisation, it remained committed to a clear concept of equality based upon a disciplined, well-organised and united labour movement. It aimed to ensure that the fruits of economic growth were enjoyed by the mass of the population. Through progressive and high levels of taxation major reforms in all areas of welfare were enacted. The state gradually extended its influence to all areas of social and economic life.

Martin Linton, in an excellent comparison of the British and Swedish labour movements (Linton 1985), put the success of the social democrats down to a number of interlocking factors. Good organisation, he claimed, had ensured the maintenance and involvement of a strong membership. The SAP has over 1,200,000 members out of a total population of eight million people. One quarter of the membership were individual members – the same *number* as the Labour Party in a population of 55 million. Three-quarters were collectively affiliated members from the trade unions. Although proportionately this figure was similar to trade union membership in Britain, the difference was that such members in Sweden had full participation and voting rights within the SAP. Trade union membership, then, took an individual form since members were involved directly in the party at every level. The result was that there was no need for separate trade union involvement at party conferences as there has been in the British party with its cumbrous bloc vote system. The SAP had more full-time agents than the Labour Party and in its youth section it had 150 as opposed to Labour's one. The youth section of the SAP was six times bigger than its British equivalent *numerically*. It too had been infiltrated by sectarian Trotskyites, as the British young socialists had been infiltrated by Militant, but these had been ruthlessly expelled in 1981. Linton claimed that the very size of the youth section prevented a takeover by a small sectarian group.

If size of membership was an important ingredient of success so was commitment. This was maintained by ensuring that participation in policy-making was thorough and widespread and that individual members had ample opportunity for political and trade union education through residential courses and study circles.

All this has been aided by a strategic use of state policies and resources to strengthen the democratic viability of the movement. Legislation which gave employees generally the right to leave from work for educational purposes has been used by trade unions to provide their members with industrial training and political education (Gould 1984a). All political parties which gain seats in the Riksdag (parliament) receive state aid according to the proportion of the electorate that voted for them in the previous election. Even more important, as Linton notes, subsidies to the press have, by making smaller newspapers less reliant on advertising, ensured the survival of 21 social democratic daily papers (Linton 1985: pp 18-20). If some people think that these policies are a misuse of state resources they must ask themselves whether it is better to have a democratic system in which the power of money determines the amount of influence a party has or whether it is the duty of a democratic state to ensure the maintenance of a genuine pluralism.

Add to all this the high degree of trade union membership,[1] a cooperative sector that controls 25 per cent of the retail trade and the wide ranging cultural and recreational activities of the movement and you have some idea of why the SAP has dominated government in a way that no other European socialist party has. This dominance has ensured that the fruits of a strong capitalist economy are distributed, individually and collectively in a fairer, more sensible, more socialist way than in other western capitalist societies. Part of the evidence for this is contained in the next two sections. In the first some of the main features of the Swedish system are described, while in the second comparative sources are quoted which lend support to the argument that Sweden is, by some criteria, a model welfare state.

THE MAIN STRUCTURAL FEATURES OF THE SWEDISH WELFARE STATE

Industrial relations and employment

The combination of social democratic governments and powerful trade unions has ensured that the labour movement has had a considerable impact on employment and economic policy generally. Centralised negotiations between SAF (the employers' federation) and LO which had been established in the Saltsjöbaden Agreement in

1938 brought a high degree of predictability to industrial relations and pay negotiations. LO itself pursued a solidaristic wage policy for many years to bring about a narrowing of differentials between different groups of manual workers and between manual and non-manual workers.

Through the Labour Market Board (AMS) set up in 1940 the government began to pursue its commitment to full employment through an active labour market policy. The scale of its activities has grown over the years and it inspired the setting up of the Manpower Services Commission in the UK in 1973. It is responsible for the government's virtual monopoly on employment services. It has the capacity to provide training and re-training for 5 per cent of the labour force in any one year. While it has been criticised for its early policy of encouraging redundant labour to move to areas of economic expansion, it has also taken its social role seriously and has provided considerable opportunities for handicapped workers and women. By the 1970s women were receiving almost half the training places provided by AMS and employers were being encouraged to provide employment for women by government loans and subsidies (Wilson 1979: p. 79).

In order to counteract the cyclical nature of the economy AMS has the power to delay or bring forward company investment. Companies can place tax-free profits into the Central Bank which can only be released if AMS approves the time, place and purpose of the investment. In this and other ways it can be seen that the Swedish state takes an active interventionist role not only in dealing with disadvantaged groups within the labour force but in promoting a successful economy (Philip 1978).[2]

Not only is the power of capital restricted by the state but management prerogatives have also been reduced. In the early 1970s policies were introduced to extend industrial democracy by increasing the influence of trade unions in the firms their members worked for. The proposal for wage-earner funds whereby a proportion of a firm's profits was to be put aside for the benefit of employees and managed by the trade unions strained the consensus between employers, employees and the government, that had been such a feature of the Swedish model. The funds were nonetheless implemented in 1982 and survive despite the objections of employers.

Social security

Pension reforms have resulted in many employees receiving a basic

21

Conflict and control in welfare policy

pension and an earnings-related pension (ATP) from the state, topped up by occupational pensions amounting in total to something like a 90 per cent income replacement rate. Even those who do not benefit from an occupational pension can expect a replacement rate of around 70 per cent and the state schemes are constructed so that there is a degree of redistribution in favour of the low paid (Wilson 1979: p. 26). Fifty per cent of pensioners also claim an income-related housing benefit, which is easy to claim and for which take-up is high. The combination of these benefits resulted in only 4 per cent of pensioners having to claim social assistance in 1974 compared with 57 per cent in Britain in 1976 (Greve 1978: p. 2).

Sickness insurance is compulsory and entitles the insured to 90 per cent of their income when sick. Parents can claim benefit on the same basis should they need to stay at home to nurse sick children or simply desire to stay at home to care for a child during its first four years. Although the state is largely responsible for the financing of unemployment insurance, the insurance funds are still administered by trade unions. Replacement rates here are at about the 60 per cent level. An inferior scheme exists for the minority of unemployed people who fall outside the trade union schemes. Universal child allowances exist for children up to the age of 16. The annual allowance (SEK 4800 or £480 approx. in 1986) is automatically increased for families with three or more children. Single parents receive double the allowance for their children.

The consequence of Sweden's extensive insurance system is that relatively few people need to seek social assistance. Whereas 10 per cent of the population were dependent on social assistance in the 1930s, the figure for the 1970s was 4–6 per cent (Elmér 1983: p. 179).

Health care

The state is responsible for most health care. Hospital care is provided by and large by the county authorities and is free for in-patients. Charges are made for out-patient visits to the doctor or the dentist but these charges are low. Abortions and sterilisation are free as is advice on contraception. The health care budget was over 10 per cent of GNP in 1975, twice that of the UK (Wilson 1979: p. 63). Combined with a high standard of living the effects of this expenditure are to give Swedes the longest life expectancy in the world (73.6 for men and 79.6 for women in 1983) and one of the lowest infant mortality rates (7 per 1000 live births) (*Statistisk Årsbok* 1986: pp.435 and 426).

Education

Compulsory and comprehensive education exists for all children between the ages of 7 and 16. A high proportion of young people stay on at school for three years after the compulsory leaving age, and most of them go on to some kind of further or higher education. Recent curriculum reforms have tried to ensure that education is both relevant and vocational. All school students receive free school meals (Boucher 1982).

Higher education is organised on a comprehensive basis also with six universities responsible for the coordination of all further and higher education within their regions. This integration enables many students to pursue degree course on a part-time basis and in institutions other than universities as such. Although a high proportion of young Swedes go into higher education it is difficult to place a figure on it since so many postpone entry into university courses. This is partly due to the fact that work experience itself counts as an admission requirement. In 1980, 60 per cent of undergraduates were aged 25 and above (Usher 1979).

Adult education has always been a distinctive feature of the Swedish system with political, trade union and voluntary organisations as well as local authorities organising study circles and courses for a large section of the population. Generous state funds are channelled through these organisations to finance adult education. Although religious and bourgeois party organisations receive such funds, they also ensure that the labour movement has a very important influence over the education of manual and non-manual workers (Jones 1976).

Housing

Extensive public programmes in the 1960s have created high housing standards. Modern estates are built to high standards with excellent insulation, central heating and other facilities. Overcrowding is almost non-existent. Seventy-five per cent of all housing has been built since 1940 and over 93 per cent of all dwellings have a bathroom, a WC and central heating. At the present time there is a housing surplus in many areas of the country. Good planning has ensured that the needs of pedestrians, car-users, the handicapped and the elderly are catered for.

Owner occupiers receive tax allowances and tenants housing allowances which enable the vast majority of the population to have access to good housing. Housing allowances rise the greater the rent and the number of dependent children and fall with increased income. About half of all pensioners receive a housing allowance and about 30 per cent of families with children – more than 60 per cent of families with three or more children. All of this has been achieved by extensive state regulation, provision and subsidy and a significant contribution has been made by the housing cooperative association (HSB). A national tenants association is consulted on rent increases and housing conditions (Elmér 1983 and Swedish Institute 1985).

Other public services

Social services will be dealt with more fully in the next chapter but it should be briefly stated here that the provision of services for the care of young children, the care of the elderly and the handicapped is of a high standard. Recreational facilities for young people and the general population are extensive as are cheap public transport services. The Swedish Welfare State aims to provide the whole population with a range of opportunities and services to enable all to share in a high standard of living and to live and work in a good environment. It caters not only for those contingencies in life that many other welfare systems aim to meet but also for those parts that other systems cannot reach.

Whatever service you look at you find unexpected additions. Immigrant workers can claim 240 hours of paid leave from work to learn Swedish. Working parents can get an allowance and have leave from work to spend more time with their children. Trains travelling long distances have spacious toilets with facilities for mothers to change babies' nappies. Travelling expenses can be claimed for journeys to hospitals and trips to schools to discuss children's education.

With one of the highest standards of living in the world, one of the lowest infant mortality rates and high life expectancy, low unemployment and a high degree of economic security, the virtual absence of visible material poverty, it is small wonder that Sweden has provided the rest of the world with something to admire, copy or envy.

THE COMPARATIVE PERSPECTIVE

Most of the reforms necessary to introduce the system outlined above came into force between the mid-1940s and the mid-1970s. They necessitated increased public expenditure and increased public employment. Public expenditure as a percentage of GNP grew to 50 per cent in 1974 and 65 per cent in 1980. Public employment which was barely 12 per cent of the total labour force in 1950 increased to 34 per cent in 1979 (Ronnby 1985: p. 65). Social security expenditure grew to 32 per cent of GNP in 1980 (International Labour Office 1985) and education to 9.5 per cent (UNESCO Statistical Yearbook 1977 and 1983) both greatly in excess of other countries' expenditures. A fairer comparison should perhaps exclude transfer payments and subsidies but even this shows that government final consumption as a percentage of GDP was 28 for Sweden, 20 for the UK and 10 for Japan (OECD National Accounts). Tables 2.1 and 2.2 below enable a comparison to be made with a number of capitalist countries.

Table 2.1 Social security expenditure as a percentage of GNP

	1965	1974	1980
Sweden	13.6	24.4	32.0
France	15.6	21.6	26.8
West Germany	16.5	20.3	23.8
Italy	14.8	21.4	18.2
UK	11.7	14.6	17.7
US	7.6	12.5	12.7
Japan	4.9	6.5	10.9

Source: *The Cost of Social Security*, 1972–74, 1975–77, 1978–80, International Labour Office 1979, 1981, 1985.

Table 2.2 Education expenditure as a percentage of GDP

	1970	1974	1980
Sweden	7.7	7.4	9.5 (1981)
US	6.6	6.2 (1975)	7.0
UK	5.3	6.2	5.8
Japan	3.9	5.1	5.8
Italy	4.0	5.0 (1975)	5.1 (1979)
France	4.9	4.7	5.0
West Germany	3.7	4.5	4.7 (1979)

Source: *Statistical Yearbook*, 1977 and 1982, UNESCO 1978, 1982.

Conflict and control in welfare policy

The size of the state welfare sector is not in itself an indicator of its quality. But many writers in the field of comparative research have confirmed the high quality and achievements of Swedish social democracy. Dorothy Wilson in her extensive study of a whole range of policies compared Sweden with other countries (Wilson 1979). She considered that if anything pensions were too generous but that the basic pension plus selective benefits gave the less well-off elderly a better standard of living than their counterparts in other countries. She wondered whether too much was being spent on health care and sickness insurance and questioned whether Sweden's lead in high longevity and low mortality rates was entirely due to state health care, but had to admit that in terms of indicators of inputs and outputs Sweden led the world. Even if one does concede that income level and environmental factors influence standards of health it is a tribute to the Swedish system as a whole that the whole population benefits from material prosperity and a decent environment. The high per capita income of US citizens has not ensured them of as high a standard of health as the Swedes enjoy. Anderson and Björkman (Heidenheimer and Elvander 1980) stated that Sweden not only devoted a higher percentage of its resources to health care but that international studies showed that Sweden was qualitatively superior to other countries.

Wilson was also of the opinion that although Sweden's child allowances were not much different from the UK's and while the provision of care of pre-school children compared unfavourably with that of other countries (an area in which great improvements have been made since Wilson wrote her book), the benefits for large and poor families and especially for single-parent families stood out in comparison (Wilson 1979: p. 107). Sweden also seems to be remarkable for the efficient and humane administration of selective benefits with the added distinction that low-paid workers can claim social assistance to bring their earnings up to the minimum level of the basic pension. In comparison the Family Income Supplement in the UK which gives working claimants 50 per cent of the difference between their income and Supplementary Benefit, seems positively mean.

Kemeny in his comparative study of housing in Australia, the UK and Sweden, has nothing but praise for the Swedish system and the way in which the least well off members of society can live in good standard housing. He claims that housing policy has been responsible for the fact that no 'inner-city problem' exists in Sweden. He suggests that British Labour Party housing policy is bankrupt compared with the visionary, long-term idealism of the SAP (Kemeny 1981a and b). Boucher, in his study of education policies quotes the OECD as recognising Sweden's leading role in this field also (Boucher 1982: p. 192), while Bill Jones, in a comparison of adult education in Sweden and the UK, found the former infinitely superior in terms of resources, participation rates and sheer scope (Jones 1976).

Most researchers who have been to Sweden or have made a detailed study of specific policies and comparisons with other countries find it hard to criticise the system. Wilson expressed many reservations but they were hardly criticisms. She quite obviously felt that since it was generally agreed among economists in the UK that high public expenditure impaired economic growth and that high state benefits and taxation were a disincentive to work, then the Swedish system must be heading for disaster. But as recent reports quoted below indicate, whatever economic troubles Sweden went through in the 1970s, her economy has not only weathered the storm but appears to be going from strength to strength.

Mishra, in his *Welfare state in crisis* (Mishra 1984), examines the ideological and political attacks that have been made on welfarism and comes to the conclusion that it is countries like Sweden and Austria that the English-speaking world needs to follow. He sees little hope for socialism in the short term and regards a corporatist approach as the only possible alternative to the offensive launched by the right in recent years. He states that Sweden epitomises what is best in 'welfare socialism' and that prosperity and security can best be pursued in a system where employers accept the goal of full employment as an important objective while workers accept the need for wage moderation and higher productivity. He accepts that Swedish corporatism is hierarchical and that the occupational interests of welfare producers do not always have a beneficial impact upon the development of social policy but considers that there is no evidence that any other system can remotely hope to generate the high standards associated with Swedish social democracy.

One last comparative study will be quoted and that is the one by Furniss and Tilton (Furniss and Tilton 1977) in which they describe three model systems which correspond roughly to those of the US, the UK and Sweden. The first they call *the positive state* which they themselves concede corresponds so closely to what Titmuss called a residual model, it is difficult to understand why they chose a new and inexplicable term. The positive state is concerned to provide the minimum welfare necessary for the maintenance of a healthy economy in the interests of the 'holders of property'. Unemployment

27

is kept only as high as is consistent with a high level of business activity. Always there is a concern that efficiency must not be undermined by social policy. Social insurance is accepted as a principle because it is largely self-financing, involves no major redistribution from rich to poor and is consistent with the work ethic. In other words welfare is subordinate to the needs of the economy and of employers. *The social security state* goes further and sees the maintenance of maximum full employment as an important end in itself and introduces the idea of a national minimum below which nobody should be allowed to fall – decent social assistance to buttress the system of social insurance. The state has a responsibility to meet those needs which the private economy fails to do. Citizens have rights which may transcend the interests of property holders. Lastly there is *the social welfare state* in which the idea of a national minimum is more generously conceived in terms of an overall aim of greater equality; public services and the planning of the environment ensure a generally high quality of living conditions; and decision-making is based upon the widest degree of participation and consultation possible. All this in addition to an absolute commitment to full employment and a generous social insurance system.

Since Furniss and Tilton wrote their book the UK has experienced a growth in unemployment and cuts in its welfare services that make one wonder whether it still qualifies even as a social security state. But the important thing about their work is that it tries to distinguish between different types of welfare system in a way that many radical and conservative critics fail to do. Their conclusions are supported by Castles and McKinlay, who in their critique of Wilensky, put much greater emphasis upon political factors and show that there is no inexorable logic that leads all industrial societies to devote a similar percentage of their Gross National Products to health and social security (Castles and McKinlay 1979; Wilensky 1975). Welfare systems are different and they cannot be indiscriminately lumped together either by convergence theorists or neo-marxists.

Castles and McKinlay explain Sweden's welfare achievements largely by the weakness of the political right but Furniss and Tilton emphasise four different traditions all of which they claim have had an effect upon the development of a welfare consensus in Sweden. A paternalism among employers, a Christian ethic of charity towards the disadvantaged, a secular tradition of rationalist planning which emphasises a preventative approach to social problems and lastly the socialist ideology of the labour movement with its emphasis upon equality and solidarity. Combined these have provided the 'moral

The Swedish welfare state

foundation of the welfare state in Sweden' (Furniss and Tilton 1977: p. 123).

The vast majority of writers in the field of comparative social policy, using data largely derived from the 60s and 70s came to the conclusion that Sweden was significantly different from other capitalist economies both quantitatively and qualitatively. The Swedish model had been developed in years of economic growth and widespread prosperity under the direction of a stable series of social democratic governments. Both the economic prosperity and the political stability however were to experience difficulties which as we shall see were to have an impact upon both welfare and control.

ECONOMIC AND POLITICAL CHANGES FROM 1975

Years of economic growth had enabled the Swedish government to raise contributions and taxation to finance increased public and welfare expenditure but as economic growth slowed down and an economic crisis hit all western capitalist countries in the 1970s it would seem that the Swedish electorate began to have cold feet about the increasingly socialist direction of state policies. In particular the 1976 election was fought on the issue of employee funds.

The social democrats had come up with a proposal to introduce funds which would enable trade unions not only to have a right to a firm's profits but as a result a big say in how the firm should be run. While this was undoubtedly an issue that was widely discussed it is not possible to say whether it was responsible for the return of the coalition governments of the three bourgeois parties – Centre, Folkpartiet (liberal) and Moderata (conservative) in 1976 and 1979. The irony is that not only were the bourgeois governments unable to reduce welfare and public expenditure but they were responsible for the nationalisation of more ailing firms than the social democrats ever were (*Economist* 1981).

The social democrats were returned in the 1982 and 1985 elections. In a system of proportional representation they have always managed to get a remarkable 45–50 per cent of the votes. In 1985 the conservative party suffered a severe setback while the liberals increased the size of their vote. It would seem that the Swedish people, on the whole feel that even in difficult economic times they prefer the SAP as the established party of power.

The social democrats have faced considerable difficulties since

Conflict and control in welfare policy

Table 2.3   Sweden: Parliamentary election results

Bourgeois bloc	1979 % votes	1979 seats	1982 % votes	1982 seats	1985 % votes	1985 seats
M (Conservatives)	20.3	73	23.6	86	21.9	76
C (Centre)	18.3	64	15.5	56	12.5	44
FP (Liberals)	10.6	38	5.9	21	14.3	51
		175		163		171
Socialist bloc						
SAP (Social Democrats)	43.2	154	45.6	166	44.9	159
VPK (Communist)	5.6	20	5.6	20	5.4	19
		174		186		178

Source: Adapted from Leivonhufvud 1982 and Hempel 1985.

being returned to office. The public sector deficit which for many years had been financed by borrowing has had to be reduced. In 1980–81 it had been 27 per cent of all public expenditure and rose to 31 per cent in 1982–83 (*Statistisk Årsbok* 1986: p. 242). This has meant that for some years (and for a few to come) the government has felt it necessary to cut central and local government expenditure. By 1985–86 the deficit had been reduced to 19 per cent. It would seem that even Sweden has reached the limits of how much taxation you can extract out of a capitalist economy.

Nevertheless there are many reliable indicators to suggest that the Swedish economy is still being managed effectively. Economic growth is returning, exports look healthy, productivity and industrial investment are increasing and unemployment is still low – 3.4 per cent in 1984 (*Linton* 1984 and *Financial Times* 1986). Keynesian economic principles have not been abandoned, only watered down, and the edifice of an imposing welfare state still exists. Kjell Olof-Feldt, the Finance Minister is quoted as saying, 'The conservatives want to use the economic crisis as an instrument to reduce public spending, so that they can reduce taxes, so they say it is impossible to bring down unemployment until you have done this or that. It's just a rationalisation of other objectives.' (*Linton* 1984). An article in the British *Economist* (not noted for its socialist sympathies) claims that there is no inverse relationship between high public expenditure and economic growth and goes on to explain that the Swedish government deliberately avoided the temptation to use unemployment in the battle for economic recovery. It chose instead to devalue the krona, abolish subsidies to lame-duck industries and to reduce the budget deficit (*Economist* 1987: pp. 19–24).

The author of the *Economist* article argues that far from full employment giving rise to high inflation and low labour mobility, neither is in evidence in Sweden. The Brookings Institute has apparently shown that labour mobility in Sweden is every bit as high as in the US. Because benefits are high, training places plentiful and jobs exist, employees are much more willing to accept the necessity of job changes. All mass unemployment does is to make people over a long period of time unemployable and in consequence lacking in mobility. Nor do high benefits result in large numbers of people preferring to claim rather than work. Again the very fact that the authorities can provide the unemployed with alternatives in the form of jobs, training or work experience means that they can insist that workers do not simply give up and rely on state handouts. Most people want to work; the state encourages them and helps them to do so instead of allowing them to rot in hopelessness as they do in the UK and the rest of Western Europe.

What is interesting here is our first link with welfare and control. The Swedish commitment to full employment cuts both ways. If society ensures that jobs and training places exist, individuals have a responsibiilty to make the best of them. The point of unemployment benefits and social assistance is not to allow people to lose their independence and self-respect but to ease the transition between a period of need, dependence and hardship so that they can go on to provide for themselves. There will of course be those on the left who will argue that this is just the sort of rationalising used by conservatives in other countries and that the social democrats are simply more effective at doing capitalism's dirty work. But such an argument misses the point entirely. If we look at a country like the UK we see a Conservative government that has allowed unemployment to grow and the numbers on social assistance to increase, all in the hope that such policies will make more people find work. The same government has tried to cut expenditure on some public services in order to generate tax cuts but has then found it necessary to finance the growing cost of the unemployed. Its attempts to provide training places and work experience then become frustrated by the very scale of the problem it has created for itself. How much more sensible to have full employment and quality provision for the minority that are out of work, coupled with an ideology which says that society has a responsibility towards you but you in turn have a responsibility towards it.

Conflict and control in welfare policy

CONCLUSION

In comparison with other western countries and Japan the Swedish welfare state stands out as a remarkable achievement, so much so that it can hardly be seen as yet another example of welfare capitalism. While it has had the broad support of the population as a whole, of employers, of religious groups and of those who are employed in the state apparatus, it is very much the creation of a powerful and disciplined labour movement. The SAP has dominated government since 1932 and the centralised manual worker federation of trade unions, LO, has had a powerful influence on both the state and employers.

Not only has the commitment to the welfare state, high public spending and full employment been maintained in years of growth and prosperity but it has weathered the recent years of recession to emerge relatively unscathed. It is my contention that this commitment has to do with not only a generous conception of state welfare but also a highly disciplined one. Most outside commentators have tended to focus on the former largely because they have simply described the universalistic nature of health, education and housing. Even in discussions of labour market policy the emphasis has been on the scale and range of specific policies in comparison with other countries, with the result that controlling mechanisms have been neglected or ignored. When they have been commented upon it has usually been in the context of the controlling needs of a capitalist society. As has already been implied in a brief discussion of the issue of unemployment, the analysis of control within the Swedish system is more complex than that.

The Swedish state has in fact traditionally combined a tender-minded and generous attitude towards welfare provision generally with a tough-minded attitude towards the recipients of social assistance and the social services. This will be demonstrated in the next chapter.

NOTES

1.   See Sease 1977: ch. 1 for comparative data on trade union membership. The Swedish Institute Fact Sheet on Industrial Relations suggests that 90 per cent of manual workers belong to trade unions in Sweden and 75 per cent of non-manual workers. These are very high percentages.

2. See Butt-Philip 1978 for a detailed comparison of the measures taken by governments in both Britain and Sweden, to create new jobs. Although it is now rather dated it showed clearly that the scale of most measures in the 1970s, with the major exception of regional policy, was far greater in Sweden.

CHAPTER THREE
Swedish social services

INTRODUCTION

When people refer to the controlling aspects of social welfare, they are not necessarily thinking of any one service in particular. Examples can be found in health care, education, social security, housing, social and employment services. Nor are they suggesting that control lies solely in the hands of officials and professionals. It also resides in the very nature of a wide range of policies, regulations and legislation itself. The four issues which form the basis of the case studies in part two, and which prompted the writing of this book, are however all drawn from one area of welfare policy – that of the social services. They are specifically concerned with the conflict between the voluntary principle and the compulsory principle. That is to say, they are about when and under what circumstances social services are entitled to force or compel clients to have help or treatment. Although the four case studies are contemporary, they did not suddenly arise in the 1980s. In order to understand their significance, it is necessary to examine the origin of the social services in Sweden and the lively and prolonged debate about compulsory care which led to the major legislative reforms of 1982.

What is generally known about Swedish social services is that the standard and provision of services for the handicapped, the elderly and young children is very high. The handicapped are integrated into the community. Elderly people are helped by a whole range of services to live a normal life within their own homes. The more infirm live in service houses which are purpose built so that they too can have flats of their own but within immediate reach of supporting social and medical services. Places in day nurseries and state-employed child minders have been increased to enable both parents to be employed if they so choose.

The last two decades have seen a sharp increase in resources – in terms of buildings, equipment and staffing – for these services. Only 4500 social workers were employed by social services in 1960, compared with 25,000 in 1980. In local authority recreation services the comparable figures were 78 and 2000. Psychologists and other similar professional workers increased from 7000 to 25,000. Total employees went up from 35,000 in 1960 to over 160,000 in 1975 (Ronnby 1985: p. 68 and pp. 146-7). Between 1965 and 1975 the number of home helps for the elderly grew by 65 per cent and the hours they worked by 178 per cent. According to Ronnby 25 per cent of pensioners were getting home helps in 1980. The total of children in day-care increased from 17,000 in 1960 to over 300,000 in 1980. Of all pre-school children 37 per cent were expected to have day-care places with the local authorities by 1982 and 70 per cent of those with working parents (Ronnby 1985: pp. 171 and 179). Of 7-10 year old school children with a registered need for day-care before and after school hours almost 80 per cent had places in 1981 (Elmer 1983: p. 186).

What is less well known is how social services are directed towards the most deprived members of the community who have to depend upon social assistance and those with social problems of one kind or another. This lack of knowledge or interest may partly derive from the fact that it is known that the extensive and generous nature of the rest of the welfare state and the commitment to full employment has resulted in relatively few people having to depend upon social assistance and that those that do, do so for relatively short periods of time. Indeed, John Greve, in his report on low incomes in Sweden, actually said, 'Social assistance payments play a very minor part in social policy – utilising less than one per cent of expenditure on social policy and only a small share of spending on income maintenance.' (Greve 1978: p. 2).

The fact is that the poor and deprived in Sweden evoke the same range of responses in Sweden as they do elsewhere. There are those individuals and groups who regard recipients of social assistance as layabouts and scroungers and those who regard them sympathetically as victims of social pressures and circumstances. The effect of the welfare state has been to minimise the necessity for people to rely on such benefits for long periods of time. It has also meant a positive and generous response towards the plight of those with social problems compared with other countries dominated by a repressive poor law ethic like the UK, the US and Japan, but it would be a mistake to assume that the Swedes have had no such element in the development of their social services. It would also be a mistake to assume that Swedish policies towards the poor and the deprived are unambiguously liberal, permissive and tolerant.

But to understand Sweden's distinctive approach to those beset by social problems one has to go back to the turn of the century – to a Sweden beginning the long path to industrialisation; to a Sweden used to dealing with the rural poor; to a Sweden with the problem of Nordic drinking habits. There we find a set of attitudes similar in many ways to those found in Victorian Britain.

FROM POOR LAW TO SOCIAL WELFARE: 1900–1968

Two things strike a foreign observer about the development of social welfare in Sweden. The first is that the early development of the system was quite repressive. The second is that laws and measures to deal with alcoholism had as much prominence as measures to deal with the elderly, the poor and neglected or 'depraved' children. All test-books on social welfare refer equally to child care laws, poor laws and temperance laws. As will be shown below the approach to each area has been similar and mutually reinforcing.

The poor law tradition

At the turn of the century the lower orders, their drinking and other problems were perceived first and foremost as a threat to the social order. As such they were worthy of, at best, charity and at worst punishment and chastisement. A strong, puritan work ethic was seen as something which the poor lacked and with which they needed to be instilled. The poor were responsible for the plight in which they found themselves. Given any type of assistance they would abuse it. Assistance was therefore given reluctantly. The conditions under which it was given were punitive in order to discourage all but the most needy.

Charity efforts were coordinated through the Central Organisation of Social Work (CSA) – a body similar to and in some ways modelled upon the British Charity Organisation Society. CSA was dominated by middle-class intellectuals with liberal, Christian attitudes who saw the handing out of poor relief as an opportunity to make people diligent, thrifty, and abstinent; an opportunity to make them responsible for themselves and not parasitical (Ronnby 1985: p. 253). A leading figure, Ebba Paul, told a CSA congress in 1906 a story about a man who although obviously in great need and clearly entitled to assistance, nevertheless refused to apply for it. Instead of condemning the harsh circumstances of the man and his family, or the stringency of the poor law measures, Ebba Paul was only too delighted to find someone who was prepared to suffer for the principle that it was his duty to supply for his own (Mattson 1984: p. 95).

Members of this body had an impact on social welfare throughout the first half of the century and sat on many of the boards and committees that influenced or ran welfare services. Long after the social democrats had established themselves as the governing party of Sweden, such people continued to dominate aspects of social policy (Holgersson 1981; pp. 81–93). Many of the institutions for the poor, the elderly, children and alcoholics were run by private individuals and philanthropic organisations. They were characterised by strict rules and corporal punishment and a morally repressive tone. The able-bodied poor could be moved on from one parish to another (rotegång) and even be sold off to the highest bidder (bortauktionering).

Illegitimate children were often removed from their parents and foster parents were paid to bring them up. Often such children would be traded as a source of cheap labour. The first child care law in 1902 was unique in that it made compulsory care an administrative decion rather than the legal one it is in most countries [only with the reform in 1982 were the courts given the final say (Grönwall and Nasenius 1982: p. 34)]. In other words the decision about compulsory care was largely a matter for the local authorities and one in which the courts had little say. The Act also introduced both the concept of a compulsory legal guardian for illegitimate children and of an övervakare, a supervisor of families in which children were neglected, badly treated or whose behaviour was considered immoral or dangerous. Both the guardian and the övervakare were lay persons of upright character appointed by local committees.

Early measures

The övervakare was later used in the temperance law of 1916 – a law which, in its turn was to have a lasting impact on other welfare legislation. An övervakare could be appointed against the wishes of adults whose drinking habits were either a danger to themselves or to others. Such an appointment was part of a sequence of measures or steps that the newly set-up temperance committees had to take in dealing with people with an alcohol problem. First an investigation would take place. If as a result the law seemed applicable, individuals would receive a warning; if the warning went unheeded instructions would be given; if these failed an övervakare would be appointed; and if this had no effect proceedings would be started to take the offending adults into care – into an institution for alcoholics.

The reasoning behind this approach was that the threat of stronger measures would act as a deterrent to the offending drinker – hence the nickname, 'the thumbscrew method'. Holgersson argues that those in favour of temperance had created institutions originally in the hope that alcoholics would use them voluntarily, but they were considered to be so awful that they remained empty. The only way to get them used was to force people into them (Holgersson 1981: p. 115). Another argument for compulsion was that alcoholics became so addicted to their habit that they could not make responsible decisions for themselves. It was therefore up to the authorities to act in their best interests – an argument used today for the compulsory treatment of drug addicts.

In 1918 and 1924, a new poor law and a new child care Act also set up elected local committees to deal with problem families and the poor. The thumbscrew methods were applied here also. Adults who failed to maintain their families could be forcibly placed in the workhouse as could beggars and vagrants. Nor were such people allowed to leave until they could show they were in a position to maintain themselves (Mattson 1984: p. 101). Old people whose behaviour was troublesome and disturbing could be taken com-pulsorily into old people's homes. Those in care under the Act were not allowed to vote, a decision which was reversed only in 1945 (Grönwall and Nasenius 1982: p. 36). In certain circumstances recipients of social assistance were obliged to repay the amounts they had received in benefit. These Acts did at the same time mark an improvement in the provision of outdoor relief and the quality of institutional care.

> The scope for obligatory help for the poor was widened ... 'rotegång' and 'botauktionering' ... were abolished. Institutional care was further regulated. Care for the poor could be given in their own homes, private lodging houses or institutions. Kommuns (borough or district councils) had the responsibility for old people's homes, which could also be managed by several kommuns jointly. The county authority was given responsibility for the workhouses for those who neglected to maintain their families, beggars and vagrants.
> (Holgersson 1981: p. 100)

Improvements continued to be made in the 1920s and especially after 1932 when the social democrats came to power. More emphasis began to be placed upon preventative measures and treatment, but the fundamental principles of thumbscrew methods and compulsion remained. In 1922 over 50,000 children were in care; 37,000 were fostered compared with 16,000 in 1970 (Holgersson 1981: p. 108). Institutions were gradually brought under state control and regulation, but even as late as the 1940s a famous Swedish novelist found it necessary to draw people's attention to the plight of elderly people in institutions. In the interests of 'social hygiene' the sick, the mentally handicapped and the elderly were often thrown together in the same institution. Many of the old people would have been able to look after themselves in their own homes with a bit of assistance, and bitterly resented institutional care.

What the early legislation had done was to recognise Sweden's transition from a rural to an industrial society. Poverty and social problems had been dealt with in one way by farmers and the parishes, but urbanisation and industrialisation required that welfare services be put on a wholly different footing.

Welfare in the 50s

A further bout of legislative improvements were initiated in the 1950s with a new temperance law in 1955, a social assistance law in 1956 and a child care law in 1960. Ration books for alcohol which had been introduced in 1917 were abolished. Unfortunately but perhaps inevitably this liberalising measure seemed to lead to an outbreak of heavy drinking, which, combined with a widening of the applicability of the temperance law resulted in even more individuals coming to the attention of the temperance committees. Elmér reports about 30,000 people being subjected to various measures each year in the 1940s although only about 1200 adults were in compulsory care each year (Elmér 1948: p. 283). Holgersson quotes a figure of 39,000 measures in 1954, 73,000 in 1956, 81,000 in 1966 and 61,000 in 1975. The vast majority of these were investigations, the value of which was highly dubious. Compulsory measures including the appointment of övervakare accounted for 21 per cent of all cases in 1966 and 13 per cent in 1975 (Holgersson 1981: p. 180). Grönwall and Nasenius claim that the new Act increased the amount of control that the authorities had over the lives of individuals. Even their freedom to live and work where they chose was restricted (Grönwall and Nasenius 1982: p. 49).

The social assistance law widened the grounds on which local kommuns were obliged to give assistance to people in need and made it possible to help claimants with more than the means to get shelter, food and clothing. No longer were relatives obliged to repay the authorities for assistance handed out to their kin. Some considered the new law a break with the past. No longer was the aim to frighten and deter but to give claimants a right to assistance. Others thought that continuities with charitable and punitive attitudes persisted. Certainly the regulations concerning custody of those neglecting to maintain their families remained until 1964 (Grönwall and Nasenius 1982: p. 50).

The child care law tried to reduce the numbers of children taken into care compulsorily and signalled a change in attitudes that was to result in a decline in the number of institutional placements. Parents were given greater rights to approach child care committees and know the grounds for their decisions. But the attitude that the best way to deal with children in bad environments was to remove them from their pernicious influence persisted, and both the committees and the police were given greater powers to investigate young people. It would seem that any advance in the rights of individuals was counterbalanced by increased rights for the authorities also (Grönwall and Nasenius 1982: p. 52).

Movement towards reform

The 1960s was a decade in which Sweden was seen by the rest of the world as a prototype for a mixed economy which had successfully achieved the goals of economic growth and high welfare expenditure. It was clearly true that standards in health care and housing had improved enormously. Full employment and decent unemployment insurance made it unnecessary for many to be on the dole. Better pensions, more home helps and assistance with transport made it possible for the vast majority of old people to lead independent lives. But for many progressive Swedes this success was flawed. Rapid industrialisation had taken its toll on a population that had within the space of two generations been transformed from a rural to an urban society. While many had gained from increased affluence and welfare, many had suffered in the transition. Individuals and families had been uprooted from the declining to the more prosperous regions. Internal migrants and immigrants from abroad had not always found it easy to acclimatise to the prosperous cities they had moved to.

As in Britain and the US poverty was rediscovered. Books began to appear which referred to the unfinished welfare state, and which described the conditions of the more deprived sections of society (Sjöström 1984: p. 140). In particular they often noted how Sweden's archaic poor law tradition had not yet been satisfactorily reformed. There was increasing concern about alcohol consumption and the new problem of drug abuse. There was concern about the fact that the social problems of deprived families seemed to be transmitted from one generation to the next and that welfare services exacerbated rather than solved their problems. That those whom society had given the worst deal should be forced to have treatment, forced to have övervakare, forced to have care, was seen as unjust. The social welfare laws were described as class laws since they disproportionately affected the working class. What kind of a socialism was this, reformers were asking, in which the most vulnerable were still punished for their plight? And how could you expect the deprived to take advantage of social services when all the time they felt that the threat of compulsory measures would be hanging over them?

Sweden was seen to be a welfare leader in all major social services but was regarded by reformers as a laggard in dealing with social outcasts, the rejected, the casualties of the system. In general it was felt that social work services need a complete overhaul, and in particular the issue of compulsion needed to be faced. Compulsory institutional care was seen as expensive and inefficient. Treatment was either non-existent or, where it existed, it was ineffective. Whatever the manifest rehabilitative function of custodial care, its latent function was always punitive. Open care, undertaken on a voluntary basis, was not only cheaper but was likely to be more effective, since it involved clients in a way that respected their dignity and their rights (Lindblom 1982: pp. 205 and 211).

Social work in Sweden had only begun to establish itself in the 1940s. Until that time what later became social work was either carried out by elected officials or lay people. Social assistance was often dealt with by administrative or financial personnel (Ronnby 1985: p. 254). Inevitably in its early stages, social work was dominated by a charity-oriented casework approach borrowed largely from the US. If any social theory influenced social work training in the 50s it was functionalist in tone. The task was to help people to adapt to society. The radicalism of the 60s began to turn this task on its head by arguing that there was something sick about a pursuit of economic growth that resulted in so many human casualties. It was time for social workers to act as advocates for their clients against an unjust system.

The reformers argued that family problems could not be dealt with in an isolated individualised fashion. The divided responsibility of child welfare committees, temperance committees and social assistance committees led to a fragmented approach to problems. What was needed was a unified approach to the totality of a family's problems; generically trained social workers employed by a unified social work service. Social work should not simply respond to problems and crises when they presented themselves on the doorstep but should engage in a preventative strategy through outreach and community work. Problems were there to be detected before they reached crisis proportions. Community resources and networks needed to be strengthened. Social workers should aim to influence the political and planning systems so that these responded to the needs of their clients.

In other words, exactly what the Seebohm committee in England was arguing for. But whereas the Seebohm committee spent a few years deliberating these issues with the result that the Social Services Act was implemented in 1970, the Swedes set up a Commission in 1968 which did not result in legislation until 1982.

FROM SOCIAL WELFARE TO SOCIAL SERVICES (1968–1982)

It is not unusual for reform to take this long in Sweden. Indeed most major reforms go through the same process. Education, pensions, health care had all experienced a lengthy and thorough investigation before reforms were enacted. Investigating Commissions in Sweden spend a long time collecting evidence from all interested parties and when they produce reports these are sent out 'on remiss' to those same groups for their reactions. This approach in the past had yielded thoroughly worked-out reforms which had the support of a broad consensus of political parties, pressure groups, trade unions, and local authorities.

The issue of compulsion

What was different about this particular reform was the more turbulent period that it straddled and the fact that it had to grapple with the issue of compulsion. It was a period in which the drug problem grew and problems associated with immigrants came to the fore. It was a period in which the social democrats became more radical and consensus between the parties decreased. Trade unions and employers came into conflict as Sweden's economy worsened. It was a period in which the electorate voted a coalition of the bourgeois parties into power after 44 years of social democratic governments.

Moreover the issue of compulsion proved to be a contentious one. While some opposed all forms of compulsion in the social services, many accepted that it was necessary for the young. Indeed most industrial countries have compulsory measures to take children into care either because their parents are mistreating them or because their own behaviour gives cause for great concern. Many countries have compulsory commitment for certain forms of mental illness. But Sweden was almost unique in having compulsory measures for adult alcoholics (Lindblom 1982: p. 205).

The Commission itself, at least initially did not take a particularly radical line on this issue. Many of the reformers therefore decided to combine their efforts in a Cooperative Committee for Social Welfare Questions (SSM) to press their case against compulsion and for a new vision for social services. It consisted of a number of organisations representing client groups, local authority workers, social workers and their directors, the workers' temperance association – Verdandi, students and other groups. While support came largely from groups on the left, SSM remained an alliance that cut across party allegiance and enabled liberally-minded people across the country to combine their efforts (Lindblom 1982: p. 196). As time went on LO and TCO gave their support and after 1976 increasing official support came from the SAP. Even the association of övervakare joined SSM in the 70s (Holgersson 1981). Gradually the movement for reform created a new consensus. The Minister for Social Affairs, Sven Aspling, was sympathetic and appointed four members of SSM to the Commission (Lindblom 1982: p. 195). Gradually its changing membership led to a majority in favour of reform.

In its first major report the Commission agreed on a range of reforms that SSM had fought for but still hung on to the idea that some form of compulsory care for adult alcoholics and drug addicts was necessary. But by the end of the 70s it had come out against such measures. The reformers had won. Or had they?

It is undeniable that the progressive wave had finally won clear support not only amongst the majority of members on the Commission but also amongst a number of social, political, professional and administrative groups. However the Liberal and Conservative members of the Commission were still opposed to the abandonment of compulsion for adults and indeed wanted it widened to cover drug addicts. So indeed did two pressure groups that had arisen in response to the drug problem – RNS, the National association for a drug-free society, and FMN, Parents against drugs. Moreover associations representing the courts, the police, the local authorities, the social welfare and criminal administrative boards (socialstyrelsen and kriminalstyrelsen) agreed. What is more to the point, so did the bourgeois government. 'The burden that a fixation with alcohol had placed upon Sweden's social welfare policy' (Holgersson 1981: p. 260), looked likely to continue.

The SOFT proposal

It would be a mistake to think that all the demands of the reformers and the proposals of the Commission waited upon the final report and the 1980s legislation. Already in 1970 a law had been passed to make possible a unified social services committee to replace the child care, temperance and social assistance committees (Elmér 1983: p. 65). Many social services departments up and down the country began to experiment with new approaches and methods. One proposal of the Commission that was taken on board in the 70s was that of SOFT. Literally SOFT stands for an addition to social insurance.

The idea, according to the Commission, was intended to relieve social workers of the task of dealing with cash benefits under the old social assistance law. As in Britain means-tested cash benefits had begun as a responsibility of local authorities. But whereas in Britain the National Assistance Board and subsequently the Department of Health and Social Security had begun to administer social assistance, in Sweden it remained a function of the local kommun. The Commission took the view that the administration of social assistance was too heavy a burden on social workers and that their work with clients and communities could be more effectively carried out if it could be absorbed into the national administration of social insurance.

The attraction of the SOFT proposal for the reformers was not only administrative. They felt that the experience of constantly applying for social assistance was unnecessary and humiliating for many clients. All those who applied for social assistance were treated as though they had other problems as well. Social workers had to conduct an investigation into aspects of their private lives in order to ascertain whether they needed support and treatment other than money. While such investigations might be necessary for problem families and young drug addicts, there were many others for whom financial help was all that was needed. Moreover there were those with long-term disabilities and handicaps which made their need for social assistance a foregone conclusion. Putting all clients through what were often unnecessary bureaucratic procedures was seen as another example of social control – an attempt to deter people from applying in the first place – a further archaic link with the poor law past.

Without waiting for new legislation to transfer the streamlining of social assistance to social insurance offices, some local authorities began to experiment with schemes of their own. One such took place in a district of Stockholm (Sunesson 1985). Sunesson describes the desk-bound, legalistic nature of much social work in Sweden. Not only did the law impose all sorts of procedures but kommuns added to these. The end result was a process which was often ritualistic, did little for the client and gave social workers no opportunity to use their professional skills. It was decided to reorganise the district so that an intake team became responsible for allocating claimants to either a SOFT team which administered the more routine applicants for social assistance or a treatment team, divested of its task of dealing with cash benefits. The time saved enabled other social workers to do outreach work with alcoholics, young people and the isolated. Within a matter of months 34 per cent of clients were claiming benefits through the SOFT method. According to Sunesson many of these people had been claiming benefits for years but the old system had not succeeded in helping them. It was so bureaucratic all it succeeded in doing was to waste the time of client and social worker alike.

The critics of SOFT were worried that people with genuine problems might be given an automatic right to benefit and fail to get the help they deserved. It was an example of 'social disarmament'. In consequence clients would be in danger of becoming welfare dependants because the new system had neglected to take an interest in them. Sunesson's view was that the old system had neglected such people anyway. What SOFT illustrated was that far from being an administrative issue, it was tied up with a view of social work in general. To the reformers, the old way of administering social assistance subjected too many people to the scrutiny of the authorities and made them distrustful of social workers. SOFT would give many claimants a sense of dignity and security and enable social workers to concentrate other forms of help where they were most needed.

The SOFT proposal, in the end, was not accepted by the

Conflict and control in welfare policy

government. The debate about its desirability, however, continues to rage into the 1980s and remains linked with the debate on compulsion.

THE NEW LEGISLATION

A new social services law (SoL) replaced the social assistance law; a separate law (LVU) dealt with the compulsory care of young people. Meanwhile a new Commission had been appointed to deal with the issue of the compulsory care of adults. Its proposals were accepted and resulted in a further piece of legislation concerned with the care of alcoholics and drug abusers (LVM). SoL and LVU were enacted in 1980 and LVM in 1981. All three came into force on 1 January 1982.

SoL was an example of legislation which set a framework within which social services departments and social workers could operate fairly freely without being bound by explicit instructions and regulations. In section one the overall aim was set out as follows:

> Public social services are to be established on a basis of democracy and solidarity, with a view to promoting economic and social security, equality of living conditions and active participation in the life of the community. With due consideration for the responsibility of the individual for his own social situation and that of others, social services are to be aimed at liberating and developing the innate resources of individuals and groups. Social service activities are to be based on respect for the self-determination of the individual.
>
> (Ministry of Health and Social Affairs 1981: p. 5)

As an aim nothing could be further from the ethos of the old poor law. As Paul Lindblom points out there are many measures that can be directed at those in need of assistance, but not all of them can be said to respect the integrity of the individual, in a way that the paragraph above does. What is particularly surprising is that this Act was passed by a government of the right. Moreover, much to the chagrin of the Minister for social affairs, representatives in the Riksdag from the Centre and Liberal Parties were perfectly happy with the socialist sentiments contained in the section.

The kommuns were charged with the ultimate responsibility for the welfare of people living within their areas. While it was up to individuals to seek help under the act, on a completely voluntary basis, it was the job of the kommun to go out of its way to ensure that it knew the needs of people in its area and that it created services to meet those needs. It meant providing people with economic assistance in the form of social bidrag (SB) and other forms of assistance and help. It meant providing information, advice and treatment to alleviate all types of social problems. It meant dealing with the total social needs of individuals, families and their communities. It meant involving the community in social planning. As far as drug and alcohol abuse were concerned the Act contented itself with admonishing kommuns to prevent and counteract abuse, providing information about the harmful effects of abuse and help and treatment for those who wanted it.

In a general way it charged kommuns with the responsibility to ensure that families had the support they needed in bringing up children; that resources were provided for those with behaviour problems and physical and mental handicaps. The elderly were to be given help to live in their own homes and given housing and communal facilities to enable them to lead a normal, meaningful life. Although residential and institutional care were to be provided, all efforts were to be made to enable people to survive in their own homes and within their own communities.

LVU catered for the compulsory care of young people up to the age of 18 (up to 20 where the care of social services was 'manifestly more appropriate') where:

> their health or development is endangered by lack of care or other conditions in their homes, or young people seriously endanger their health or development by abuse of habit-forming agents, criminal activity or any other comparable behaviour.
> (Ministry of Health and Social Affairs 1981: p. 35)

Compulsory care had to be approved by the county court except in the case of immediate custody, where the risk to a young person was too great for delay. Approval for this in the first instance had to be made by the chairperson of the social welfare council but the case had to go to the county court within a week of the order being made.

By and large, where people suffered from alcohol and drug abuse, social workers were to be guided by the principles set out in SoL and every attempt was to be made to ensure that care and treatment were provided on a voluntary basis. But where adequate care could not be made under this act, LVM was to come into operation. Care could be ordered where: 'People were seriously endangering their physical and mental health through the abuse or were liable to inflict serious harm on themselves or on some person near to them through the abuse' (Ministry of Health and Social Affairs 1982: p. 3).

Again it was up to the county court to grant a care order which it could only do after a suitable investigation had been made of the circumstances and on the production of a medical certificate. Care could last for two months, with the possibility of renewal for a further two months. This measure was very much a compromise that left no-one satisfied. The reformers wanted the abolition of compulsory care for adults and those that wanted to retain it preferred the old system whereby adults could be kept for up to six months. Nevertheless Lindblom felt that it was still an advance on the old temperance law. Compulsion was strictly limited; it could not be used until voluntary alternatives had been exhausted; there was no obligation on social welfare committees to use it; nor were they expected to use it if appropriate treatment could not be provided (Lindblom 1982: p. 208).

DEVELOPMENTS SINCE 1982

Before moving on to the case studies in Part two we need to briefly consider events subsequent to the new legislation. Because of the unease about how the new laws would work out the bourgeois government appointed another Commission in 1980 to watch over future developments and to make further recommendations if necessary. The re-election of the social democrats in 1982 should have ushered in a new era for the social services with their new philosophy and rationale. Unfortunately the period has been dogged by the need for the government to reduce public expenditure in general and in the social services in particular. It has also been significant in that the person chosen to be Minister for social affairs, Girtrud Sigurdsen, should turn out to be someone who thought that the 1982 reforms had gone too far.

Sigurdsen's contribution to the evolution of social services in Sweden, in the eyes of her opponents has been to take a few steps back into the past. She has introduced the idea of 'mellan-tvång' or intermediate force and is seeking to strengthen the compulsory elements in LVU and LVM. Mellan-tvång is a term used to describe the measure introduced in 1985 enabling social services committees to appoint an individual to supervise a young person thought to be in need of care. Inevitably an association is made with the idea of compulsory övervakare. In order to alter the LVU and LVM laws she has changed the composition of the Commission appointed in 1980, so that it will take a less progressive line. In the summer of 1987 the Commission proposed a lengthening of the time limit for the compulsory care of adults from two to six months. Part of the justification for this was the emergence of the AIDs problem and its association with drug abuse.

Moreover she has let it be known that she opposes the SOFT reform on ideological not administrative or financial grounds. She quite clearly believes that to allow too many people an automatic right to SB will lessen the amount of control over clients that social services departments and their social workers have at present.

CONCLUSION

What is difficult to understand for an Anglo-Saxon observer is the concentrated nature of Sweden's historical development. It is as though two centuries have become compressed together. On the one hand there is a repressive poor law tradition similar to Britain's in the nineteenth century. On the other hand there is a labour movement which advances the development of the welfare state more quickly and more ambitiously than any other industrialised country. In Britain, the ending of the poor law and the beginnings of a welfare state overlap but not to the extent that they do in Sweden. In British social policy there is a continuity of ideas, attitudes and policies that can be traced back to the past, but in Sweden this continuity is concentrated within the space of three generations. This makes the Swedish welfare state even more remarkable and in some ways difficult to explain.

It is undeniable that over the years there has been a liberalising of Sweden's welfare policies and provision. Institutional care has been reduced and improved. Means-tested social assistance has become less stringent and less stigmatising. People with problems are more likely to be seen as victims in need of care and treatment, rather than as parasites and criminals who deserve punishment. But this liberalisation has always been met with a degree of resistance and at times in recent years it has seemed as though the tide was turning. Sweden remains a society in which compulsory care is used not only for adult alcoholics but drug addicts as well. It remains a society in which it is felt by some that other forms of compulsion are used too readily. It remains a society in which the conditions under which social assistance is given by some local authorities are very strict.

Conflict and control in welfare policy

In British social policy we explain harsh and repressive attitudes in social policy by emphasising the strength of the right in British politics, and the conservatism of the British working class. But Sweden has consistently elected progressive social democratic governments supported by a powerful trade union and cooperative movement. The Swedish working class and indeed the Swedish population as a whole have embraced the concept of the welfare state in a way that British socialists and social democrats can only envy. And yet many Swedish writers explain the elements of control and compulsion in social policy in terms similar to those that we would use in Britain.

It is clear then from this cursory examination of the development of social services in Sweden that the debate on compulsion has a history that goes back to the turn of the century. Compulsion has its origins in Sweden's poor law and is associated with class repression. But it also has links with the temperance movement and the desire to control alcoholism. It has been attacked by reformers, many of whom have been associated with the labour movement. It has been supported by the right and the institutions of law and order. But I think it would be a mistake to see this conflict as a simple dispute between the left and the right. The present role of Girtrud Sigurdsen shows that the situation is a little bit more ambiguous than that. As we shall see from the case studies, there are many on the left – local politicians, social workers and activists and not simply those in government – who would like to see more restrictive policies and a return to a greater emphasis upon control and compulsion in the social services. The question then becomes one of how we explain such divisions. Part two will present the political conflicts, while Part three will attempt an explanation of them.

Conflict in the 1980s: Four case studies

CHAPTER FOUR
Children in care

INTRODUCTION TO THE CASE STUDIES

The following case studies demonstrate the persistence of the conflict concerning control and compulsion in Swedish welfare policy into the 1980s. The fact that they are about the care of children, social assistance and drug and alcohol abuse, mirrors each of the traditional divisions of the social services. The material upon which the case studies are based consists of official statistics and reports; social work journals, books and newspaper articles; interviews with central and local government personnel, academics and representatives of relevant pressure groups. The first concerns the numbers of children taken into care.

'THE STATE THAT SNATCHES CHILDREN'

Whether a particular country takes too many or too few children into care is a difficult and complex issue to examine. If individual cases are examined after the relevant decisions have been made, it can be argued that hindsight can in no way compensate for the involvement in the actual events, emotions and circumstances that existed at the time; written records and recollections are no substitute for the real-life dramas and crises that the children, the parents and the social workers experienced. If overall statistics are compared with other countries then it can be said that they are objectified artefacts that conceal enormous differences in social problems, social work education and practice and legal and administrative requirements and regulations. Nevertheless, serious allegations are made from time to time about the way in which social services neglect or too eagerly pursue their responsibilities. Controversies arise and these have somehow to be discussed and analysed. New social services laws which were intended to resolve the debate on compulsion came into force in Sweden early in 1982, and soon afterwards such a controversy arose. In this case study the circumstances surrounding this particular controversy are examined and statistical comparisons are made both historically and with other countries, in order to find out if there was any truth in the allegations that the Swedish authorities took too many children into care and if so, why. It will be argued that although the allegations would seem to have been exaggerated by particular pressure groups, there does seem to be a strong relationship between children being taken into care and the problems of drug and alcohol abuse. In a country with a strong temperance tradition, it may well be that there is a greater temptation to remove children from their families when such abuse, either by the parents or even the children themselves, is suspected, than in countries without such a tradition.

ACCOUNTS IN THE BRITISH MEDIA

Just before the British General Election of June 1983 an article appeared in *The Times* which argued that disproportionately large numbers of children were taken into care in Sweden (Brown 1983). Similar articles appeared in the *Observer* the following October and in August 1984 (Mosey 1983 and 1984). Further articles in the *Daily Mail* and the *Spectator* were subsequently traced as well as a Radio Four programme broadcast by the BBC (Brown 1981 and Hale 1983). The headlines themselves give an indication of the tone of the articles – ILL FARES THE WELFARE STATE, SPECTRE OF CHILDREN'S GULAG HAUNTS SWEDEN and THE STATE THAT SNATCHES CHILDREN. Given that Sweden generally merits little attention in the British press, this was wide coverage indeed for what might be considered a minor welfare issue. In the first article a 1979 figure of 30,000 children was referred to, where the authorities had made some sort of decision regarding their protection and care. By comparing this with the number of children born in Sweden annually as being in the order of 90,000, the article claimed erroneously that this meant that 'every third child born in Sweden can expect to become of interest to social workers during their childhood'.

This led to the conclusion that 'between *five and ten times* as many children are taken from families by the Swedish state than in any other comparable country' (my italics).

In the *Observer* articles a figure of 24,000 was referred to while the BBC programme was content with 20,000. The *Observer* compared the Swedish figure with 162 in Norway, 710 in Denmark and 552 in Finland. No wonder the BBC programme claimed that 'Sweden holds the world record for the number, more precisely the percentage of children taken into custody'.

The reasons advanced for these allegedly high figures were many. It was said that young, inexperienced, under-trained social workers were guided by half-baked psychological theories. They were employed in large numbers by the state which then gave them ample resources to terrorise the Swedish citizenry. Moreover the vagueness of the law enabled social workers to use the flimsiest of evidence to snatch children away from their parents. Gossip and suspicion seemed sufficient justification for state interference. A number of lurid and plausible cases were then cited to illustrate a picture of an authoritarian state apparatus which rode roughshod over parental rights. As an earlier article in the *Daily Mail* put it:

> Sweden is of course the country which has so frequently been paraded before us as the socialist paradise – proof that socialism and freedom are not uneasy bedfellows. But ... it is the one country in the world where the riches produced by a capitalist economy enable social workers to treat the family as arbitrarily as the countries of eastern Europe would like to if they could afford to. Sweden is not politically totalitarian. But is social totalitarianism, of which the child care authorities are only one example, any better? (*Daily Mail* 1981)

Now the details of the cases themselves would be very difficult to check up on. They are indeed very frightening, if true. But the accounts only presented the views of the parents and did little justice to those of the social workers. Indeed, the most publicised case was alleged by Andrew Brown, upon further examination, to be totally misleading and almost fictitious. Brown wrote an honest recantation in the *Spectator* but this did nothing to correct the general impression that the mass-media had already created (Brown 1984). One is entitled therefore to be somewhat suspicious about the other illustrative examples used by the journalists. One might also have had suspicions about those articles that appeared in Conservative newspapers criticising *the* welfare state especially the one that was published just

Conflict and control in welfare policy

before the election. The fact that the general tone of the articles was reinforced by the more liberal *Observer* and the BBC, however, suggested that the issue was worthy of further investigation.

The first stage of doing so began with an examination of statistical evidence, both historical and comparative; the second consisted of a series of interviews with pressure group representatives in Sweden in the summer of 1985; while the third involved a re-evaluation of this evidence in the light of material collected more recently.

STATISTICAL EVIDENCE

Historical comparison

The historical evidence can be found in an article by Sten Johansson (Johansson 1980). In spite of legislative and statistical changes, particularly in 1960 and 1969, he felt that the figures and trends over time were comparable. Figure 4.1 shows the rates of children in care from 1928, according to whether the children were brought into care with their parents' consent or compulsorily, or were subjected to preventative measures. The latter consisted of the series of warnings referred to in Chapter 4 which culminated in the appointment of an övervakare, a sort of lay probation officer (also see Chapter 5). As will be mentioned later, the nearest equivalent to these preventative measures in British social work practice are supervision orders which do not appear in our statistics for children in care. It is also important to note that the rates here refer to the 'flow' of children in care throughout a given year and not to the 'stock' at a point in time.

It can be clearly seen that the rate of voluntary cases has steadily declined from the mid-1930s, from nearly 20 per 1000 of the population under 21, to less than five per thousand. Johansson attributes this to the reduction in material poverty and the decline of serious illnesses such as tuberculosis which caused many parents to be unable to look after their children. The rate for compulsory cases of care hovers at about 4 per 1000 between 1940 and 1960, and between 4 and 5 per 1000 between 1960 and 1978. Johansson's figures therefore give no cause for alarm as the trend over half a century seems to be down.

However, a closer examination of the official statistics from 1971 reveals some interesting details (Table 4.1). In the decade from 1971 to 1981 total measures declined from 40,000 to 30,000. This decrease was

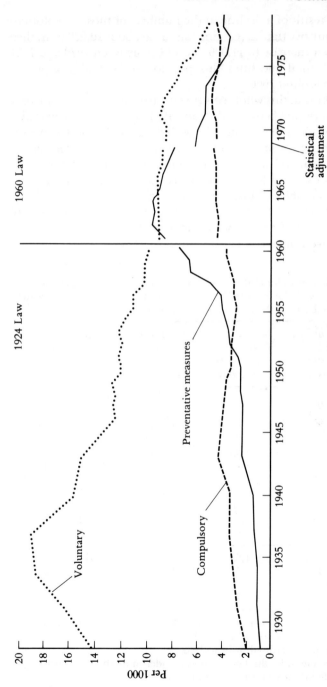

Figure 4.1 Total per 1000 of the population under 21, from 1928 to 1978, subject to voluntary care, compulsory care or preventative measures according to child care legislation
Source: Johansson, S. *Barnens Välfärd*, Institutet för Social Forskning, Stockholm, 1980

Conflict and control in welfare policy

largely the result of a decline in the numbers of those in voluntary care. Compulsory figures remained steady at about 10,000 until there was a sudden increase to 11,000 and 12,000 between 1979 and 1981. From 1982, total measures dropped to 26,000 and compulsory measures to around 7000.

Could it be that this whole controversy arose because of an increase in compulsory care between 1979 and 1981? If so what is interesting about the period is that it coincides with the second period of office of the bourgeois government and the last years of the old legislation. The subsequent and dramatic decline in both the total measures and compulsory cases could therefore be seen as partly a consequence of the new, more liberal legislation and a reaction to the outcry in the press in 1983 and 1984. What is perfectly clear is that the increase took place three years after the social democrats left office and that their return to government coincided with the decline.

Table 4.1   Measures for children and young people according to the old Child Care Law (BvL) from 1971 to 1981, and the new Social Services Act (SoL) and the Law for the Care of Young Persons (LVU)

	Preventative measures[1] contact person	In custody for investigation[1]/ immediate custody	Voluntary care	Compulsory care	Total measures[2]
1971	12,245	1,570	19,706	10,559	40,622
1972	12,220	1,525	19,244	10,820	40,480
1973	12,027	1,401	18,091	10,891	39,482
1974	10,646	1,314	16,884	9,960	36,038
1975	9,273	1,357	16,101	9,730	33,738
1976	8,233	1,524	13,948	9,700	30,601
1977	7,984	1,506	13,002	9,836	29,578
1978	9,033	1,618	12,237	10,187	29,870
1979	9,601	1,869	11,357	10,942	30,278
1980	10,387	1,971	10,403	11,802	30,853
1981	10,841	1,605	9,483	12,378	31,067
1982	7,280	1,034	11,837	9,944	26,820
1983	6,489	879	11,839	7,718	24,319
1984	6,926	755	11,490	6,951	23,683
1985	7,698	755	11,490	6,399	23,693

Sources: Beslut om åtgärder enligt barnavårdslagen 1980/81 Insatser för barn och unga enlight SoL och LVU 1982–85

Notes (1) Categories used prior to 1982.
 (2) Some individual cases appear under more than one heading. Total measures is a net figure.

58

Although the 1979–81 increase was too small to justify the foreign press's more outrageous claims it could have been significant enough domestically to produce a great deal of concern. But were those who were part of that outcry entitled to claim that Sweden compared badly with other countries? In order to find out a comparison between the official Swedish statistics and those of England and Wales was made.

Comparison with England and Wales

Although Sweden differs in many ways from the UK, it seemed reasonable to compare its statistics with those of England and Wales (figures for Scotland and Northern Ireland are compiled separately) for a number of reasons, not least because British journalists had already implied that Sweden's performance was so outrageous. Although Sweden is twice the size of Britain geographically and has only 14 per cent of its population, nevertheless both countries are advanced capitalist economies, with a high degree of political centralisation; both are parliamentary democracies and have constitutional monarchies; both have a welfare state and a strong labour movement.

The legal background to child care measures in both countries is at first sight rather complicated. Prior to the 1980s a number of different laws governed the procedures by which children could be taken into care. The Child Care Act of 1980 consolidated the law for England and Wales, while the Swedes did the same with the Social Services Act of 1982 (SoL and LVU). Nevertheless it was possible for the years I had chosen for comparison (1979–83 – the years immediately preceding the media coverage) to distinguish clearly between voluntary and compulsory care for both countries.

One important difference was that young offenders in Sweden were almost entirely dealt with by the social welfare authorities and with the exception of a small number of 15–17 year olds (20 in 1982) all those taken from their homes were included in the statistics for children in care. As will be pointed out later, an adjustment needs to be made to the English and Welsh figures to include young people sent to detention centres to make the two countries strictly comparable.

In both countries children could be taken into care either because of parental neglect or abuse on the one hand or because their own behaviour suggested that they were in need of protection. The law in both countries had, to use Anna Hollander's terms, moved from the concrete to the abstract (Hollander 1985), or from the specific to the general. The Swedish law, for example, stated that compulsory care was to be provided for young people if 'their health or development is endangered by lack of care or other conditions in their homes' (Ministry of Health and Social Affairs 1981). Compare this with the English Act of 1980 which says that a local authority may resume parental rights where a parent 'is of such habits and mode of life as to be unfit to have care of the child' (Holden 1980).

In the Swedish context, Hollander was worried that vague formulations of the law would give rise to a 'superficial unanimity' among local authority and judicial personnel (Hollander 1985) and lead to unjust decisions. Jean Packman, a leading British authority, however, has insisted that 'A degree of ambiguity in child care policies allows room for the vital exercise of discretion, without which a sensitive and "personal" response would be impossible' (Packman *et al* 1986).

Whatever one's views on this matter there seems to be a rough similarity between the laws of the two countries.

Before we look at the statistics, two further points need to be made. Prior to 1982, Swedish figures only distinguished between the *flow* of care measures in operation throughout a particular year (i.e. all those still in care from previous years plus all those who came into care during the course of the year) and new cases admitted during that year. The former would give a rather misleading impression when compared to child care rates in other countries such as England and Wales because rates are calculated here on the basis of the *stock* of children in care *on a particular day of the year*. The second point is that Swedish figures include 'preventative measures'. As mentioned before, prior to 1982 these included 'warnings' and the imposition of a person called an övervakare. The övervakare was a sort of lay probation officer who could not only be imposed on a family but had an obligation to report to the welfare committee should the child's or the parent's behaviour warrant it (see Chapter 5 and Socialstyrelsen 1985). The 1982 Act replaced the övervakare with the 'contact person or family'. A contact person could not be imposed upon a client, and had no duty to report back to the committee. His or her task was to befriend and support the client. The nearest equivalent in England is the supervision order, whereby a social worker can be given the responsibility to watch a child or family closely, by law. The point is that the supervision orders do not appear in the English and Welsh statistics, but if they were taken into account they would have the same effect as preventative measures and contact persons have on the

Children in care

Swedish figures. These two points have been taken into account in order to make the figures for the two countries comparable.

The comparison shows that the proportions of children in care on a particular day of the year are very similar. Consistently from 1979 to 1983, the rates for both countries were about 7.7 per 1000 of those under 18 years of age (Table 4.2). Nor is there much difference between the two countries in terms of the percentages of those who came into care voluntarily (i.e with the permission of their parents) and those who came into care compulsorily (Table 4.3). The proportions for both countries were approximately 45 per cent voluntary and 55 per cent compulsory. The proportions were reversed for Sweden in 1982 and 1983. What is clear is that in no sense can it be said that a larger proportion of Swedish children are compulsorily removed from the family.

Table 4.2 Children in care on 31 March (England and Wales) and 31 December (Sweden) per 1000 of those under 18, 1979–83

	1979	1980	1981	1982	1983
England and Wales	7.7	7.8	7.6	7.5	6.7
Sweden	(7.9)*	(8.0)*	(7.7)*	7.3	7.5

Sources:
(1) Children Care in England and Wales, 1979–82 Department of Health and Social Security.
(2) Children in Care of Local Authorities Year Ending 31 March 1983, England, DHSS.
(3) Beslut om Åtgärder enligt Barnavårdslagen 1979–81
(4) Insatser för barn och unga, 1982–3, Statistika centralbyrån
*Estimates based upon the ratio of children in care on one day, to children in care throughout the year, derived from statistics for 1982–3.

Table 4.3 Voluntary and compulsory routes into care. Percentages 1979–83

	1979	1980	1981	1982	1983
England and Wales					
Vol.	45	44	43	43	42
Comp.	55	56	57	57	58
Sweden					
Vol.	47	43	41	53	55
Comp.	53	57	59	47	45

Sources: As for Table 4.2.

Conflict and control in welfare policy

Rates of new admissions to care were also looked at. A difficulty here is that prior to 1982 Swedish rates were published per 1000 under the age of 20. English and Welsh figures have always been published per 1000 under the age of 18, as indeed have the most recent Swedish rates. For the years where they are most comparable, it would seem that again there is a remarkable similarity – around three per 1000 (Table 4.4).

Table 4.4 New admissions to care per 1000 of the population under 18* 1979–83

	1979	1980	1981	1982	1983
England and Wales	3.1	3.3	3.1	3.0	2.5
Sweden	2.3*	2.3*	1.9*	2.7	3.0

Sources: As for Table 4.2.

The most important differences that could be found, related to the duration of care and the form of placement. Sixty per cent of English children were in care for less than a year compared to less than 40 per cent in Sweden. Only 25 per cent of English children were in care for more than three years whereas the figure for Sweden is more like 45 per cent (Table 4.5). While around 50 per cent of English cases were placed in foster homes, in Sweden the figure was almost 90 per cent (Table 4.6).

As has been mentioned already, the comparison with England and Wales has been made because British journalists had implied that

Table 4.5 Terminated cases of care by length of care. Percentages 1979–83

	1979	1980	1981	1982	1983
Less than 6 months					
England and Wales	54	53	50	53	54
Sweden	31	29	24	33	43
Less than 1 year					
England and Wales	58	58	56	58	58
Sweden	40	38	32	40	53
More than 3 years					
England and Wales	24	25	26	26	25
Sweden	41	43	44	48	32

Sources: As for Table 4.2.

Table 4.6 Family homes as a percentage of total placements

	1979	1980	1981	1982	1983
England and Wales	45*	45*	49*	53	57
Sweden	87	87	87	87	88

*England only
Sources: Children in Care of Local Authorities Year Ending 31st
March 1979-83, England DHSS
For Sweden: Beslut om Åtgärder enligt Barnavårdslagen 1979-81
Insatser för barn och unga, 1982-3, Statistika centralbyrån

Swedish rates were much higher than those of other countries. The figures on children in care do not seem to be anything like as bad as suggested. Not only would Sweden seem to be similar to England and Wales in its child care rates but if you accept that the Swedish figures include many young people who in this country would be in detention centres and borstal training then an adjustment to the rates to take this into account would leave Sweden in a more favourable position. In 1982 custodial sentences for young people under the age of 18 came to 7,200 (Criminal Statistics for England and Wales 1982) which would imply an increase in the child care rate for England and Wales for that year of 0.5 – taking it from 7.5 to 8.0. There would therefore seem to be some justification for the claim by the Swedish Ministry for Health and Social Affairs that Swedish child care rates are similar to those of the US and Western European countries generally (Ministry of Health and Social Affairs 1983).

Comparison with other Nordic countries

It could be argued however, that Sweden should not be compared with a declining economy like the UK, where there is more family poverty, higher unemployment, a more congested population and chronic inner city problems. What do we find then if we compare Sweden with its Scandinavian neighbours? A comparative analysis published by the social welfare ministries of Sweden, Norway, Denmark and Finland (Nordisk Ministerråd 1985) showed the following (Table 4.7).

The first point to make is that these figures bear no resemblance to those quoted above from an article in the *Observer*. Secondly, Swedish figures compare well with Denmark's (indeed in the previous year, 1981, the Danish rate was higher than the Swedish) and

Conflict and control in welfare policy

Table 4.7   Children in care in the Nordic countries.

	Denmark	Finland	Norway	Sweden
Numbers of children in care throughout 1982	14,523	8,888	4,600	20,649
Children in care throughout 1982, per 1000 of the population under 20	10.3	7.7	3.9	10.0

Source: *Barnevern i Norden*, Nordisk Ministerråd, 1985, p. 88.

not too badly with those of Finland. Only in comparison with Norway can it be said that the Swedish rate is high. Indeed for a number of years the Swedish rate has been two and a half to three times as great as the Norwegian rate. The representatives of the Scandinavian ministries explained this difference between Norway on the one hand and its neighbours on the other by saying that Norway had a more dispersed population, stronger family ties, and a lower incidence of alcoholism, suicide and divorce (Nordisk Ministerråd 1985).

One might equally argue therefore, on the basis of population density and social problems generally that Sweden's rate should be lower than that of England and Wales and closer to that of Norway. On the other hand the Swedes do have a higher suicide rate and may well experience, although they are difficult to compare, higher rates of divorce and alcoholism (see Chapter 7 for statistics on alcohol problems).

A tentative conclusion from an examination of the statistics must be that the media articles referred to at the beginning of this chapter exaggerated greatly. It simply cannot be said that the Swedish rate of children in care is between five and ten times that of 'any other comparable country' or that Sweden 'holds the world record' for the rate of children in care. Nevertheless it is possible to understand how the increase in compulsory cases between 1979 and 1981 might have caused some alarm and there would seem to be some justification for supposing that the figures in Sweden should be lower than Britain's and closer to those of Norway. Moreover children do seem to be kept in care for longer periods in Sweden. The subsequent stages of this investigation sought to discover why specific groups and individuals within Sweden itself found it so necessary to exaggerate what might otherwise have been a more plausible case.

A PRELIMINARY EXAMINATION OF SWEDISH SOURCES

Concern about the numbers of Swedish children in care had been expressed internationally, not just by the British media. Pressure groups and individuals within Sweden had brought the issue to the attention of the international media. In the summer of 1985 a visit to Sweden was made to discuss the issue with many of those who had supplied the world's press with arguments, statistics and case details. The interviews were designed to discover how groups and individuals perceived the problem and its causes and how they thought it could be solved. But in the course of these discussions the politics of the issue also became apparent.

In particular, it became clear that a rather roundabout strategy had been used to bring the issue to the attention of the Swedish public since the Swedish press had not shown a great interest in the issue. Two groups, RFFR (The Family Rights Association) and FK (Family Campaign) decided to feed information and stories to foreign journalists. When the issue had been given sensational coverage in West Germany's *Der Spiegel,* in Britain and other countries, the interested parties back in Sweden were able to claim that Swedish welfare practice was so bad that it had aroused international criticism. As a publicity technique this was ingenious if somewhat misleading. The internal concern in Sweden was relative to a whole range of legal, social and political issues which were never mentioned by the foreign press. Sweden's poor performance compared with other countries was always implied but never demonstrated. If the British articles were anything to go by no attempt was made to ask what the situation in the journalists' own countries was like. In other words Swedish pressure groups had implied an adverse comparison; foreign journalists accepted it without question; and as a result the Swedish people were alerted to a major defect in their welfare system which other countries were supposed not to have.

The motives of foreign journalists for attacking the Swedish welfare state were many, no doubt, ranging from a crusading desire to tell the truth to doing whatever pleased the political whims of their editors. But the motives of the Swedish participants in this debate also merit some scrutiny, since they emerge from the publicity as simple champions of the underdog against the massed forces of the Swedish state.

Family Campaign[1]

Politically, FK was quite obviously to the right and seemed to specialise in moral and political panic. In British terms it was closer to the Festival of Light than the Family Policy Unit. Founded in 1969 FK was concerned that the family was threatened with extermination by the policies of a socialist government, influenced by marxists and radical feminists. It saw a whole generation of Swedish youth as being corrupted by alcohol, drugs and video-violence. The result was vandalism, suicide and a shrinking birth-rate, for which the socialist welfare state was responsible.

Its argument was that high welfare expenditure required high rates of taxation which made two-income families a necessity. Mothers were forced out to work by a combination of high taxes and punitive social assistance rules. Their children had to be left in state-run nurseries where they were indoctrinated by left-wing ideology. The overt concern of FK was that mothers should have the right to choose whether or not they stayed at home to bring up their children. FK had only recently become concerned about the children in care issue. It argued in similar vein, that parenting was being eroded by welfare experts. When people applied for social assistance, they and their homes were vetted by social workers. When children reached the age of four, they were forced to undergo physical and medical tests. All this surveillance meant that unconventional parents came under the scrutiny of hyper-critical welfare professionals more often than in other countries. FK argued that part of the solution was to give social workers a Christian training in place of the marxist one they received at present, but that the real solution to the problem lay in drastically cutting back welfare state expenditure. This would result in tax cuts which would enable families to survive on the male breadwinner's wage and thus allow mothers to choose to stay at home to look after their children.

While some aspects of these arguments deserve serious considera-tion, if not investigation, their conspiratorial and ideological tone ought to give rise to some suspicion. One is entitled to ask whether FK was likely to be scrupulous in its selection of evidence and case material, or whether, given its libertarian stance, it would be tempted by any opportunity to attack the social democratic concept of the welfare state.

The Family Rights Association[2]

RFFR's membership spans the liberally minded from the centre to the left. It was founded in 1981 at Barnbyn Skå, a therapeutic institution which treats whole families on a voluntary basis. Leading figures in

RFFR include Sven Hessle and Bengt Börjesson, both of whom have
worked for the institution and are now academics in university social
work departments. Barnbyn Skå has an international reputation for
its radical and progressive approach to family therapy.

RFFR saw separation from the biological family as traumatic for
both the parent(s) and the child. It was felt that the prevailing policy
in state social work emphasised the need to quickly remove children
from inadequate environments and place them in good ones. Given
the predominance of fostering as a form of care in Sweden, this meant
finding good foster homes. RFFR was sceptical of the value of
fostering and felt that much more should be done to ensure that
children stayed with their families of origin. In particular it was felt
that much more could be done by working with and supporting the
parents, enabling them adequately to take care of their children.
Where fostering was unavoidable, much useful social work could be
done (a) at the separation stage (b) during foster care and (c) when
children were being returned to their real parents, to ensure good
contact, understanding and liaison were maintained.

RFFR was arguing for a new set of priorities in social work that had
implications for social work training and practice and a different
allocation of resources. It was thought that more social workers
would be required to work intensively with clients in the early stages
of family problems; more small institutions would be required,
similar to Barnbyn Skå, as well as crisis centres. The argument
maintained that this did not necessarily imply an increase in
resources but that by concentrating on problems in their early stages,
and through preventative work, the long-term costs of inadequate
care could be avoided. When the present head of Barnbyn Skå was
asked whether there were any follow-up studies to demonstrate the
effectiveness of the therapy and experiences there, he said there were
none. As to whether intensive social work in the early stages would
result in savings in expensive fostering later, that requires an act of
faith that social service policy-makers could be forgiven for doubting.
It is ironic that RFFR has begun to provide the very back-up support
to parents that it has suggested the state should provide. Through its
network of local organisations, with some financial support from the
state, the Association now provides volunteer support for families
who are experiencing or who are likely to experience care proceedings.
As a voluntary organisation it probably does a better job at protecting
people's rights than a state agency, already a party to the dispute,
could do, and more cheaply.

While RFFR was able to quote many examples of parents who had been given a raw deal by social workers and the courts, it was not able to demonstrate that Sweden had a disproportionate number of children in care. Hessle claimed in one article that, 'Over 20,000 children are in care in our country today. It is a large number even by international comparison ... Over half those in care are there compulsorily, which stands in stark contrast to other countries' (Hessle 1982). Since he went to the trouble to make his point one would have thought that he would have supplied the comparative evidence, but he did not. '20,000' and 'over half' sounded big and convincing, so he rested his case. RFFR's present position is that it is concerned not so much about the numbers taken into care as with the whole business of how custody is handled.

Within the Swedish policy-making community it would seem that RFFR was trying to encourage a new set of priorities; new ways of thinking about problem families and new ways of working with them. Its members did indeed believe that many children were taken into care unnecessarily. However, at this stage of my investigation I was inclined to believe that the device of involving foreign journalists had been a gimmick. After all the latter would not have been interested in a debate about social work methods nor in the fact that there was a domestic disagreement about the numbers in care. They would only have been interested if it could be shown that Sweden was somehow unique. The way chosen was to concentrate on the arbitrary authority of what was supposed to be a caring state and claim that the numbers in care compared very unfavourably with other countries.

This view was reinforced by interviews with others who offered variations on the argument advanced by RFFR. Some criticised a general tendency in Swedish culture in favour of order; child care policy was a facet of a more general desire to keep the streets clean. Others blamed the lofty and perhaps unrealistic expectations of welfarism, that all social problems had neat, administrative solutions. For some the law was too vague and was biased in favour of the authorities; for others it was a question of inexperienced and inadequately trained social workers who were too busy administering social assistance from behind bureaucratic desks to dirty their hands by actually working with families. Common to all these arguments including those emanating from Barnbyn Skå, was an anti-bureaucratic, anti-professional, anti-state streak that one tended to associate with the libertarian left.

At this stage of the investigation it seemed that the controversy about the numbers of children in care had been exaggerated by FK and RFFR. The libertarian arguments of a right-wing and a left-wing pressure group had combined in an attack upon what were seen as the authoritarian tendencies of the welfare state. While such arguments must be respected as legitimate criticisms, similar ones have been made of all examples of state welfare, and might not therefore indicate that there is anything particularly wrong with the Swedish system.

The defenders of the system[3]

Those interviewed who defended Swedish policies on children in care did in fact imply that the problem had been exaggerated for political and ideological reasons. They claimed that the evidence used by the critics had been highly selective and sensationalised. Although journalists had no compunction about exploiting people's stories, social workers could hardly reply, given that their answers would not only betray confidentiality, but also damage their clients. As far as comparisons with other countries were concerned, it was said either that the statistics were not comparable because of differences in the laws and their application or that they were compiled in different ways. Even where they were comparable, it was suggested that different countries tackled their problems in different ways and that whereas in Sweden, children exposed to danger were properly regarded as the responsibility of the state, other countries were simply not as conscientious. In Norway, young children could be found late at night on the streets of Oslo; in Berlin there were child prostitutes while in England we took risks that resulted in the deaths of children who should have been in care.

There was no attempt to disguise the fact that Swedish society faced many problems which made children vulnerable. The increase in both parents working, in divorce, in one-parent families, led to problems which resulted in stress, alcohol or drug-abuse and neglect. There were problems associated with the migration of labour, both internal and from abroad. The welfare state had solved the problem of material poverty, but affluence, economic change and commercialism had created others.

The tone of such defences suggested a degree of pride in Sweden's welfare superiority. It seemed as plausible to argue that other countries took too few children into care as to say that Sweden took too many. It was only after the next stage of the analysis when it was possible to connect this issue with the debate on control and compulsion generally that things became clearer.

'CHILDREN'S NEEDS AND PARENTS' RIGHTS'

As already mentioned at the end of the last chapter, even before the major reforms in the social services had been enacted at the beginning of the 1980s, the bourgeois government had set up a new Commission to keep an eye on developments, with a view to making further recommendations if necessary. In 1986 it produced a report entitled, *Children's Needs and Parents' Rights* (SOU 1986: 20 and 21) which proposed a new law on the compulsory care of young people (LTU) to replace LVU.

The report is a very thorough discussion of the evidence, arguments and events surrounding the issue of children in care in the 1980s. In great detail it set out to examine the opposing schools of thought claiming from the start that its intention was not to make compulsory care more difficult but to clarify and make more precise the wording of the old Act where experience had shown this to be necessary. The end result, however was quite clearly very close to what RFFR and those who opposed compulsion in general would have wanted to see. The report made clear that underlying the conflict were fundamentally different ways of looking at the development of young children. The *needs-oriented* school claimed that children and their parents did not always have the same interests and that where these came into conflict the state had the responsibility to look after the interests of the children. When biological parents did meet the needs of their children it was in the interests of all that families be helped to stay together but where abuse and neglect by parents prevented children's needs from being met, it was time to think of substitutes for the biological parents. Good foster parents might be able to give neglected children what their inadequate biological parents could not. Linked with this approach was a tendency to regard children as having a discrete set of instincts, drives and needs that required satisfaction and to look for well-defined indicators as to the adequacy of parents. It was suggested that this school of thinking had had a considerable impact on the policies of many local authorities.

In contrast the *relations-oriented* school claimed that the factors involved in the relationship between children and their parents were complex. To look at specific needs or indicators out of context was to underestimate the degree to which children became emotionally bound to their biological parents from infancy onwards. To separate children even from parents who ill-treated them quite badly might do more harm than good to all concerned. Separation should therefore be seen as an absolutely last resort. It was much more important to give biological parents the help and support they needed to cope. Should separation be necessary, all efforts should be made to maintain the relationship between the children and their real parents with a view to re-uniting them at some point in the future.

The report went on to examine the evidence for both of these positions but came to the conclusion that much of it had been pre-determined by the theoretical starting points of the researchers (SOU 1986: 20, p. 104). Nevertheless it was clear from a number of comments about the cost, inefficiency and ineffectiveness that most of the members of the Commission were inclined to reject the needs-oriented model. The final proposal stated that the new law should take into account not only the child's need for care but also for secure relationships and that where separation occurred every effort should be made to maintain contact between parents and their children and to ensure that they were re-united as soon as possible.

It was felt that social workers had abused the LVU category of 'Immediate Custody' and that this should therefore be replaced by the term 'Temporary Custody'. The intention of the former was to provide social workers with the possibility of taking children into care in emergency situations which could not wait on the slow deliberations of committees and courts. It was suggested that this had been used as a short-cut to compulsory care and that the new paragraph should clearly state the temporary nature of the measure. A similar abuse of section 28 of SoL was stopped. This had enabled the authorities to prevent a child in voluntary care from returning to its parents if it was thought that this was unwise. Thus what parents had agreed to as a voluntary measure could become compulsory without the cumbersome procedures that compulsory care demanded. It was also proposed that social welfare councils should have to demonstrate that they had done everything they could to try to provide support and help within the child's home on a voluntary basis before making a request to the courts for compulsory care; that parents and their representatives should be given greater opportunities to comment on any investigations into or decisions affecting their families; and that cases of compulsory care should be reviewed every six months.

These proposals went a long way to meeting the demands of RFFR and those who generally believed that there had been too great an emphasis on compulsion in Swedish social services. They also met the criticisms of researchers like Anna Hollander (Hollander 1985, 1986) and Ulla Bager-Sjögren (Bager-Sjögren 1984) who had independently examined a number of cases of compulsory care in a variety of local authorities. Hollander had concluded that the existing legislation was too vaguely worded to protect the rights of parents or children *vis-à-vis* the authorities while Bager-Sjögren believed that many local authorities had not given parents either the legal support required by the legislation, the opportunity to be involved in the deliberations leading up to the care decision, or the chance to maintain links with their children while they were in care.

But the proposals were not to everyone's liking. Members of the Commission disagreed amongst themselves and Girtrud Sigurdsen, the Minister for Health and Social Affairs refused to send the LTU proposals out on remiss until a legal expert appointed by her had had the chance to review LVU in the light of the commission's proposals. As a result two sets of proposals were sent out on remiss in the summer of 1987.

One interesting objection to LTU came from Britt Persson in the first issue of a new social work magazine (Persson, B. 1987) in which she restated the case for protecting the interests of children which she claimed should not be seen as identical to those of the parents. In doing so she made two points which are worth bearing in mind when we come to consider later case studies and the way in which we should interpret them. One concerns her use of the concept of an underclass and the other the use of indicators in the detection of child abuse.

One of Persson's objections to the Commission's report was that to her there seemed to be no consideration of the socio-economic factors that brought about the problems that led to the need to take children into care. Instead there seemed to be too great a willingness to attack the institutions and personnel that had been set up to deal with the problems, i.e. social services and social workers. Even the little consideration the report gave to background factors was flawed, she said. The report implied that working-class people were over-represented in cases of compulsory care. This, Persson claimed, was an exaggeration. She insisted that the official categories (Class 1, professional and managerial; class 2, intermediate non-manual; class 3 manual and routine white-collar workers) were outdated and illogical and were widely recognised as such. But more to the point class 3 consisted of many people who, she claimed, were not members of the working class at all. They were, in fact, rejects from the working class, and should, she asserted, be more appropriately categorised as an underclass.

This is mentioned because a similar argument has been used by socialists like Jan Myrdal to advocate tougher measures against drug abuse. He argued that drug-users, thieves and prostitutes were reactionary members of the lumpenproletariat (underclass) and as such had been used historically by capitalists to undermine the workers' struggle for a better social order (Lind and Hartelius 1982). Presumably Persson, in regarding many of the families, whose children were in care, as being members of an underclass, also considered them as obstacles to a better social order. This would then link with her argument about the use of indicators in the detection of child abuse.

The report had said that although indicators like alcohol and drug abuse and mental disturbance should be seen as signals that all may not be well within a family, they should not in themselves be used as reasons for taking children into care. Persson argued that the commission was ignoring the fact that research had shown that such indicators were indeed strong grounds for intervention. The fact was that although it was sometimes said that too many children were taken into care: '... I would turn this about. Too many children in Sweden suffer. Mental illness, alcohol and drug abuse, mistreatment and sexual abuse are elements in the lives of too many families and their children' (Persson, B 1987). This had led her earlier to say: 'Many children live under unacceptable conditions and children need a stronger protection of their rights... we can be proud that we in Sweden have a law which protects children' (Ibid). It is clear from this that much of the argument about the use of compulsory care hinges upon the attitudes that those in the social services have towards indicators such as alcohol and drug abuse with one side insisting that they are almost a reason for intervention in themselves and the other saying that they are merely a signal. The Commission obviously felt that it was conceivable that a parent might abuse alcohol or drugs yet remain a good parent with family relationships worth preserving; to its opponents this was inconceivable.

ALCOHOL AND DRUGS AS INDICATORS FOR INTERVENTION

The sort of research that Britt Persson was referring to is typified by a study by Rydelius of the children of alcoholic fathers (Rydelius 1981). Rydelius carried out a follow-up study of 229 adults who 20 years previously had been the subject of an investigation into the physical and mental health of 4–12 year old children, whose fathers had attended the Maria clinic for alcoholics. The initial study in 1958 had shown how the children had suffered mentally and physically from the abuse and neglect of their fathers. Twenty years on, Rydelius found that the 'boys' (now young men) were more likely to be on criminal, alcoholic and child care registers than a matched control group whose fathers had not been alcoholics. Moreover the young men were also more likely to have been recipients of social assistance, sickness benefit and health care. This led Rydelius to conclude that alcoholic parents should be used by psychiatric clinics to identify children at risk.

That this was in fact done, and done indiscriminately by social workers, was alleged by RFFR in a seminar held in Stockholm in 1983. The report of the seminar claimed that:

> Syringe and bottle stir up inexorable fantasies in the minds of many of slums inhabited by drug addicts and blind-drunk alcoholics. For the general public, politicians, social workers and experts it is obvious that the children should be taken into care. Research also shows that the chief motive behind compulsory care, if one goes to the case files, is drug and alcohol-abuse. Between a quarter and two-thirds of the chief reasons social workers use to take children into care, are alcohol and drug-abuse in families. In parts of our large cities such abuse is almost the sole reason. In Gothenburg for example, over two-thirds of compulsory care cases are alcohol and drug abuse cases.
>
> (RFFR 1983: p. 2)

Sven Hessle followed this by saying that to take many of these children away was to further damage the parent who was addicted, even more fundamentally, and to condemn their children to a life in the care apparatus of the state, from which they would emerge as the criminals and misfits of the future (RFFR 1983: p. 6).

I have already suggested that RFFR, as a pressure group, pushing a particular line might be prone to exaggeration. Certainly the figures referred to above had no references whereby one might check their accuracy or otherwise. But I did examine the research carried out by Hollander and Bager-Sjögren into custody cases and the results were as follows. In the Bager-Sjögren study alcohol and drug abuse represented 43 per cent of the main indicators (Bager-Sjögren 1984: pp. 67–9). Hollander's larger sample gave a figure of 40 per cent, but when this overall figure was broken down for the three years 1974, 1977 and 1982 from which her cases were derived, the figures showed a distinctly upward trend – 28, 47, and 50 per cent. Given that these figures include local authorities in small and medium-sized towns as well as one large city, they tend to support Sven Hessle's claim.

All that we can conclude from this is that the abuse of drugs and alcohol forms the principal reason for taking children into care in

Sweden. We cannot say whether the intervention was necessary or desirable. Nevertheless, given Sweden's preoccupation with the subject there are good grounds for believing that the whole society tends to react strongly to the problem of alcoholism and drug-abuse (see Chapters 3 and 7). Supporting evidence for this assertion can be found in a previous report by the Commission into psychiatric care.

The report shows that whereas in Denmark and Norway the proportion of mental patients undergoing compulsory care are, per 100,000 of the population, 26 and 109 respectively, in Sweden the figure is 248. The report adds that a large proportion of these are alcoholics and drug addicts (SOU 1984: 64, pp. 158–9). The Swedish figure is also high compared to England where the rate for compulsory admissions is only 36 per 100,000 of the population (DHSS 1985). All this would seem to suggest that any excessive use of compulsory care measures generally in Sweden is directly linked with the preoccupation with alcohol and drug-abuse.

CONCLUSION

The allegations that Sweden takes a disproportionately large number of children into care seem to have been exaggerated both by the world's press and by pressure groups within Sweden itself. Nevertheless comparative figures do suggest that for a small, wealthy society with a fine welfare state the rate is quite high and the duration of care rather long. This is reinforced by the figures which show that there was a rise in the number of compulsory cases at the end of the 1970s which may have been the cause of the domestic concern which sparked off foreign interest. There are also good grounds for supposing that Swedish society and institutions are particularly concerned about the problems of drug and alcohol-abuse and that this may therefore lead to a greater concern for children in families where such abuse takes place, than would exist in other countries.

On this particular issue, there would seem to have been a concerted attack by pressure groups from the left and the right of the political spectrum upon what were seen as the authoritarian tendencies of the state. In view of this loose alliance between forces of the left and right, it is also interesting to note that the authoritarian tendencies under attack were as much in evidence when the bourgeois government was in power as they would seem to be now with a social democratic minister in charge of social affairs. For this reason, it is plausible to advance the hypothesis that the debate in Sweden about the controlling aspects of welfare policy might be as much a conflict between authoritarians and libertarians as between the left and the right.

NOTES

1. This description of Family Campaign is partly based on an interview with one of its leading organisers, Katarina Runske, but also on some of its publicity material.
2. This section is based upon an interview with two prominent members, Ingmar Böcker and Gail Watt, as well as publicity material; and upon interviews with a researcher for Stockholm's Social Services Department; a head of section in Malmö's Social Services; a member of the Commission investigating LVU; and a former and present Head of Barnbyn skå.
3. Based upon interviews with two Stockholm social workers, two journalists, two researchers at the Institute for Social Research, Stockholm University and a representative of Rädda Barnen (Save the Children).

CHAPTER FIVE

Preventative measures: support or control?

INTRODUCTION

The Social Services Act of 1982 (SoL) was a watershed in Swedish social policy in more ways than one. It was an attempt by the reformists to break with a past that to their way of thinking had relied far too much on compulsion and control. The previous chapter has shown that SoL, through its emphasis on voluntary measures, was intended to reduce the numbers of children coming into care compulsorily. As we have seen the numbers have indeed declined, and in part this must be attributable to the philosophy of the new Act. But care orders were not the only compulsory part of the old child care legislation. Certain preventative measures could also be imposed upon a family without the consent of the parents. Parents would be *warned* about certain behaviour; if it persisted they would be *ordered* to see that it stopped; if it carried on an övervakare would be appointed to supervise the family; and finally if all these measures failed the child might well be taken into care. These measures were included in the annual statistics and Table 4.1 shows that they declined from 12,000 in 1971 to around 7000 in the 1980s. The reason for this decline was that SoL abolished the systematic steps of warnings, orders and supervision. Their place was taken by a purely voluntary, preventative measure – that of providing the support of a contact person (CP) or contact family (CF). In keeping with the rest of the Act, preventative measures moved from the compulsory to the voluntary, from control to support.

This case study begins with a brief discussion about preventative measures generally and then goes on to describe the use made by Swedish social services of övervakare and contact persons. This

introduces a survey carried out by the author in Karlskoga and
Örebro, which consisted of interviews with contact persons, clients
and social workers. The survey shows that by and large, the transition
from 'compulsory' övervakare to 'voluntary' contact persons has been
successful, but that it might be aided further if the organisation of
contact persons could be removed from social services departments.

PREVENTATIVE MEASURES

The concept of prevention in social policy is very wide. In a sense the
whole battery of welfare services provided in a society can be called
preventative. They exist to prevent 'squalor, ignorance, disease,
idleness and poverty' – Beveridge's five giants. Even a care order is
preventative since it is intended to prevent harm to a child. In a
narrower sense we can assume it to mean measures which are taken to
prevent the problems within a family from deteriorating to a point
where a care order may be necessary. But even with this definition it is
possible to distinguish measures which range from support to
control.

If we think of a single parent struggling to bring up three young
children, there are a number of ways in which social services in the
UK could help her. Efforts might be made to provide places for the
children in a day nursery. She might be given support in the form of a
home help or a family aide employed by the local authority, to enable
her to cope with domestic tasks. If an item of essential furniture was
lacking, social services would find a way of providing it. The children
might be provided with a holiday at the expense of the local
authority. A voluntary organisation like Homestart might be
approached to send one of their helpers into the family. In short there
are many ways in which a family can be given help in the form of
cash, goods or services, by statutory and voluntary agencies, which
may be regarded as preventative support.

If we think of another family where a child has been badly treated
but after a period in care has been allowed to return to his parents, a
social services department might seek a supervision order from the
courts to enable a social worker to keep a close watch on the family to
ensure that the problem does not recur. This too is preventative but in
a much more controlling way.

Swedish social workers have a similar array of measures to offer a
family with problems but there is a much greater reliance upon state

as opposed to voluntary provision. Many of these measures, like their British counterparts do not enter into the statistics concerned with children in care. But others do, in particular statistics on övervakare prior to the 1982 Act and CPs and CFs since the Act came into force. An understanding of what these people did, or do, and how they have been used, is important to an understanding of the dilemma between support and control, and between the voluntary and compulsory principles that underlie Swedish welfare policy. It will also tell us something about the relationship between the state and the use of 'voluntary' helpers in Sweden.

ÖVERVAKARE

Övervakare were created by Sweden's earliest child care law in 1902. In the legislation concerning 'the upbringing of depraved and morally-neglected children' the child care committee was empowered 'To find a suitable person to follow the child's living conditions and supervise his upbringing and give advice and assistance for this upbringing' (Svensk Författnings-Samling: 1903).

Temperance committees were given similar powers for the treatment of alcoholics in 1913. In 1918, the criminal code adopted the same idea and övervakare became lay probation officers.

> The övervakare has to carry out the supervision of the sentenced person and seek to promote what will redound to his correction .... During probation, the sentenced person shall carry on an orderly life; avoid bad company; try to find the means of support in an honest way; and keep the övervakare informed of his address. If summoned, he should place himself at the övervakare's home and not absent himself from a visit; answer his written messages without delay and take heed of his advice and warnings. Nor should he remove himself from his place of work without first having sought the övervakare's advice.
>
> (Svensk Författnings-Samling 1919)

The policy of using övervakare continued into the 1970s and is still used in criminal care. There is now a National Association of Övervakare and Contact Persons (ÖKR). Although there has been some modification of the övervakare's role over the decades, it has remained an explicit form of social control and as such became a source of embarrassment to the reformers. However, it is fair to say that the övervakare association played a progressive role in the debate

Conflict and control in welfare policy

on compulsion in the 1970s and has criticised what it sees as the numbers of mentally ill people detained in Sweden (ÖKR 1985).

CONTACT PERSONS AND CONTACT FAMILIES

Although CPs and CFs had been used by a number of local authorities during the 1970s, it was SoL which gave them legal recognition. It states in section 10 that a social welfare committee: 'may appoint a particular person or family to help the individual and his next of kin in personal affairs, if the individual requests or consents to such an arrangement' (Ministry of Health and Social Affairs 1981). The emphasis on consent is very important as can be seen from the guidelines issued by Socialstyrelsen and Svenska Kommunförbundet (The National Board for Social Welfare and the Swedish Association of Municipal Councils), in a booklet entitled 'An Ordinary Person' (Socialstyrelsen 1985). In it they made clear the difference between the old-style övervakare and the new concept of a CP.

It stated that övervakare could be appointed against the wishes of a client. There was a strong element of control in their work and they had the responsibility of reporting back to the old child welfare committee. CPs and CFs on the contrary, could not be appointed against a client's wishes; they were there primarily as a support for the client and they had no obligation to submit reports either to social workers or to the new social welfare committee. They should not be seen as controllers, as the extended arm of a social worker or as a resource for investigation. The booklet went on to describe what the Board and the Association regarded as good practice, based upon the experiences of some local authorities in both Sweden and Norway.

It suggested that CPs and CFs could be used in a variety of situations but that they should not be used for severe problems. Recruitment could be through advertisements placed in newspapers or through contacts with voluntary organisations and trade unions. Applicants should be invited to an informal interview to find out if they were suitable for the work. They should be mature people with no great problems of their own. They should have a degree of stability in their own lives; be law-abiding and not have extreme views. Prospective CPs and CFs should then be invited to attend a study circle to discuss the nature of contact work. Such a study circle could also aid the screening process and ensure that unsuitable candidates were eliminated. Those regarded as suitable should then be invited to attend further study circles, say two four-hour sessions in which social problems, welfare agencies and the function of CPs and CFs could be explored.

When those selected were put on a local authority register of contact workers, the next task was to ensure that a particular contact worker was suitable for a particular client. Care should be taken to choose someone not too distant from the client, either socially or geographically. A meeting should be arranged to enable a client to judge for him or herself whether the contact worker was suitable. Such a meeting should be arranged on neutral premises or in the client's home, but preferably not in the offices of social services. Having been chosen, the contact worker should then come to an agreement with the social worker about the nature of the tasks and responsibilities to be undertaken. The aims should be clear and limited. It was important that a contact worker should not be expected to deal with the problems of a whole family, nor was it necessary for a contact worker to know more about a particular family or individual than was necessary for the carrying out of their task. The agreement should also specify the necessity for confidentiality and details of hours to be worked and compensation.

Once contact work had begun, the guidelines continued, it would be necessary for the social worker to keep a check on what was going on. Support and supervision should enable a social worker to know whether the work was being carried out adequately or not, and to decide whether it should continue. An evaluation session should take place every three months with all three parties present to ensure that nothing went on behind the client's back. Rarely should it be necessary for contact work to last for more than two years. Contact workers should have the opportunity to meet and discuss their work with each other every so often and at the completion of a particular case they should be able to discuss with the social worker how the work had gone.

It is important to add to this summary of the guidelines that contact workers are paid. They are not employees of the local authority in any formal sense, but neither are they strictly speaking, volunteers. Although there is some variation from one local authority to another, most stick closely to the nationally recommended scales. In 1986 a CP in Örebro could receive between SKR 195 and SKR 430 (£20 and £43) a month depending on the nature of the commitment. In addition there would be a standard SKR 195 for expenses. CFs who looked after children at weekends could also claim SKR 57 per person per night and travelling expenses. These amounts are not particularly high if you take Sweden's high cost of living into account (as a rough guide a British pound will buy in Sweden only two thirds what it will buy in the UK) but they ensure that contact workers are not out of pocket as a result of the work they do. What is important is that they are paid directly by the local authority for work which in the UK would in all probability be carried out by unpaid volunteers.

The trouble with official guidelines such as the ones described, is that while they may give social workers some helpful hints and some examples of good practice they have a tendency to gloss over the reality and ignore many of the practical obstacles and problems. And in complying with the spirit of new legislation they may fail to recognise the possibility of old practices continuing in spite of what the law says. It seemed to me that the idea of contact workers was, in itself, admirable. It tapped the altruism of ordinary people, while ensuring that they were not out of pocket; it was an inexpensive use of non-professional, community-based resources; it freed social workers for more professional tasks and gave support to people who lacked resources and networks of their own. But was this what happened in practice? And was there perhaps an element of the old övervakare in all this? Was this a gentler way of keeping tabs on people with social problems? Were CPs and CFs primarily a support for the client or were they agents of social control?

THE SURVEY

In the spring of 1986 a grant from the Nuffield Foundation enabled me to visit Sweden to pursue these questions. After discussions with Swedish colleagues it was decided that a sample of CPs, CFs, their clients and the clients' social workers drawn from the kommun of Karlskoga and the district of Vivalla-Lundby in the town of Örebro, would be interviewed. Both areas are situated in Örebro county which lies midway between Gothenburg and Stockholm. Karlskoga is a small town of 35,000 people whose fortunes depend upon the viability of Bofors, a large manufacturer of weapons. Over 7000 are employed by Bofors out of an employed labour force of 19,000. Fifty per cent of the work-force are employed by manufacturing industry, while 25 per cent are employed in the public sector. Another 18 per cent are employed in other services. In 1983 when unemployment in Sweden as a whole was 3.5 per cent, in Karlskoga it was 5.8 per cent (Karlskoga 1985).

Örebro is a large town of 117,000 people. Like Karlskoga it is a kommun but because of its size it is divided into 15 districts, one of which is Vivalla-Lundby with a population of just over 8000. Whereas Karlskoga has one social welfare council which is responsible for social services throughout the town, each of Örebro's districts has a council responsible for all kommun services including social services. Only 18 per cent of employees are employed in manufacturing; 43 per cent are employed in the public sector and a further 31 per cent in other services. In 1983 unemployment in Vivalla-Lundby was 4.9 per cent – slightly higher than for Örebro town as a whole. However, these figures are slightly deceptive since Vivalla-Lundby is an administrative area consisting of two contrasting estates. Vivalla is a public housing estate and preponderantly working-class, while Lundby is largely owner-occupied and middle-class. This is illustrated by figures for those on social bidrag (SB or social assistance). In the first three months of 1986 17 per cent of households were in receipt of SB, but 90 per cent of these lived in Vivalla. It is Vivalla which has a disproportionate number of single parent families, unemployed people, drug addicts and alcoholics (Örebro 1984).

This also explains why there were 30 CPs and CFs in a small district of Örebro while there were only 44 in the whole of Karlskoga. From the sample of 74, one in three was randomly selected for interview, together with the clients for which they were responsible as well as the clients' social workers. This was important because the responses of one group would act as a check on the responses of the others, particularly on questions concerning control and effectiveness. Out of the sample of 24 cases, 23 CPs and CFs responded and 19 clients. Fourteen social workers, responsible for 21 of the cases, responded. Of the remaining social workers one was on strike and one sick at the time the interviews took place.

The appointments for interviews in Karlskoga were arranged by senior social workers and took place in social work offices. In Vivalla-Lundby, most of the interviews with CPs, CFs and clients, took place in their own homes and the arrangements were left to me. The location of the interviews did not seem to affect the responses of individuals, although it might be argued that those that took place in social work offices might have created the impression that I was acting in an official capacity. However that was probably overcome by the obvious fact that I was a researcher who lived in and was employed in another country. This was made clear in advance by the social workers and by me at the beginning of every interview.

Conflict and control in welfare policy

The aims of the survey were firstly to discover how far contact work in reality corresponded to the model set out in the booklet outlined above, and secondly to assess how far CPs and CFs were agents of social control. Before presenting the results, it is necessary to consider the responses of those social workers who either had the responsibility of organising contact work or who knew something about the way it was organised in their respective areas.

Contact work: the seniors' point of view

In Vivalla-Lundby, one senior social worker had the responsibility for the recruitment of CPs and CFs. In Karlskoga there was no one person responsible either in the central office or in the three district offices. The following is based therefore upon interviews with Vivalla-Lundby's organiser, Karlskoga's Director of Social Services and three senior social workers representing the south, east and west districts of the town. Their views were remarkably similar and corresponded largely with the official view described above.

They confirmed that the shift in policy had preceded the 1982 Act but that the Act itself had been of great importance. CPs and CFs were different from övervakare in that they were voluntary and did not have a duty to report formally to social services (except in cases of child abuse where there was a generalised requirement in Swedish law that all citizens had a moral obligation to report such matters). They were very much a support for the client and neither an agent for the social worker nor a controlling force. The whole idea was that people with problems of addiction, loneliness and difficult relationships should be able to rely on an ordinary member of the public, not associated with the authorities. It was important that clients did not feel that CPs and CFs were going to social workers behind their backs and betraying confidences.

Recruitment in Vivalla followed more closely the lines laid down by Socialstyrelsen, in that they not only had an organiser who kept a list of all available contact workers and recruited for all the social workers in the office, but they also advertised in newspapers and delivered leaflets through doors in an attempt to attract people. In Karlskoga, the policy seemed to be to leave it to individual social workers to find someone suitable when the occasion arose. While this seemed to work satisfactorily it did result in a greater reliance upon the old list of övervakare. Vivalla, on the other hand, did not seem to find it necessary to have formal agreements in all cases whereas in Karlskoga this was the norm. Both however claimed to arrange meetings between all three parties at the outset. It was difficult for them to say how often contact workers met with clients and social workers subsequently since it varied so much, but there seemed to be an agreement that they should meet at least every six months. There was agreement too on the main aim of such work which was to help the client function better in normal everyday life, and that by and large, such work was successful. Such an aim was achieved, according to the organiser in Vivalla, by 'Together, training the client in the skills lacking; for example – planning finances, getting up at a reasonable time in the morning, going to work and staying there all day, cutting off bad friends and making new, better ones, finding new interests and occupations to grow, to make your own life' or as one of Karlskoga's seniors put it, the aim was 'To share activities together such as sports or visits to the cinema, to talk, to get clients to use their own resources, to look after the children and enable the mother to have free time.' More CPs and CFs were needed but this was not because of a lack of resources to pay them. The cost to social services was minimal (0.12 per cent of Karlskoga's 1986 social services budget – Karlskoga 1986) and they had money for more. What was difficult was finding the time to organise the recruitment of suitable people and resources for training. This was true for both areas.

Characteristics of those interviewed

The principal difference between CPs and CFs was that the former were assigned to particular individuals with special problems, usually a parent, teenager or an adult; whereas the task of the latter tended to be to look after young children one weekend in every three or four in order to give the parent(s) a respite. As far as the interviews were concerned, however, the contact family was always represented by the wife, never the husband, and never the two of them together. It is unlikely that this was intentional on the part of those who were responsible for informing the CFs about the interview. It is more likely that it was simply another example of the fact that it is women who tend to take (or have thrust upon them) the major responsibility for caring activities.

Of the 23 contact workers most were married women, between the ages of 30 and 50; 6 had had higher education, while 9 had left school at the earliest opportunity; 13 were employed full-time and 5 part-time. Of those not employed, 1 was a housewife, 2 were pensioners and 2 were students. When asked about their present and previous occupations, it turned out that 18 had been employed in the field of welfare generally – 12 as ancillary workers, 6 as professionals – and 4 as other white-collar workers. Of the 19 clients, 16 were women, most of whom were single parents in their 20s and 30s; none had had higher education and most were manual or routine white-collar workers. Twelve of the 14 social workers were also women in their 20s and 30s, most of whom were married and all of whom were qualified social workers who had been to university. The three groups were similar in that most of them were women, but different in terms of age, education, occupation and marital status; with the clients younger, least educated, mostly working-class and single parents. The concentration of contact workers in welfare occupations does suggest that the scope for recruitment is rather narrow and limited.

CPs and CFs

Most of the contact workers had been doing contact work for over a year and had only one client at a time. Only one had received any training for the task and only two had experienced group work; all three agreed that this had been useful and valuable. All found the work interesting and satisfying and only six found it stressful. When asked why they had become involved in contact work, half said it was because they were interested in, and wanted to help, people; three had done it because it was useful experience for their future employment, while the rest simply said it was because they had been approached.

Nine of the sample had been övervakare, most of whom were CPs rather than CFs and from Karlskoga. As with the concentration in welfare occupations, this does rather suggest a narrowness in recruitment especially given the distinction the authorities have wanted to make between the work of the old övervakare and their modern counterparts. As might be expected, the clients were described as having a number of problems ranging from the single parent situation and general behaviour problems of both parents and children, to specific problems connected with finance, alcohol and drugs. Drugs or alcohol were mentioned in 9 out of the 24 (37.5 per cent) cases by either the CPs, CFs or social workers; a figure only slightly lower than that described for child care cases in the previous chapter. It is interesting to note that the interview contained no specific question on drug or alcohol problems and that these were sometimes mentioned by either the contact worker or the social worker but not both. It is therefore possible that the proportion of clients with such a problem is understated.

Aims were expressed generally in terms of alleviating these

problems and by and large the respondents thought their work was successful in doing just that. Although in a few cases it was felt that extra help was needed, contact work was thought to be an appropriate response to these problems. It would seem that, as intended, contact work was being used for modest problems that could be assisted by non-professional people. Much of their work simply involved being with and talking to the client but CPs, in particular, stated that they accompanied clients on visits to public authorities and recreational trips. Many helped with financial problems and a few helped clients find work or educational courses.

Although in most of the cases it was social workers who suggested the idea of a CP or CF to the client, in 7 the initiative came from the client. In 14 of the cases the clients personally chose the person they wanted. In 5 cases there was no initial meeting for the client to get to know the contact worker. In the 18 where there were, 6 took place in the social services department or another welfare agency, while the rest took place in the homes of the clients or the contact workers. While, on the whole, this conformed to the practice recommended – that such meetings should take place and preferably not in welfare agencies – a significant number did not.

Moreover, in 5 cases there were no written agreements – all of them in Vivalla-Lundby, and in those cases where there were, few contact workers could remember their aims and tasks being specified. Most agreements seemed to state when contact workers should meet for supervision sessions with the social worker and details of hours to be worked, fees and expenses. The number of occasions when client and contact worker met subsequently and the amount of time spent together, varied enormously from one case to another (see Tables 5.1 and 5.2).

Contact work and the issue of control

Twenty of the respondents claimed that their foremost loyalty was to the client. Except for a few in Karlskoga, they certainly did not see themselves as agents of control or of the social worker. They saw themselves, as the legislation intended, primarily as a support for the client. Asked about the difference between themselves and övervakare they certainly thought there was one, but only nine were able to define it satisfactorily in terms of the voluntary and the compulsory nature of their responsiblities.

A number of questions sought to elicit their attitudes to reporting their clients to the authorities. In answer all of them said they did not

Conflict and control in welfare policy

Table 5.1 Frequency with
which contact workers met with
clients

less than once a month	1
once a month	6
twice a month	7
once a week	4
twice a week	3
more than twice a week	2
Total contact workers	23

write reports, nor did they feel legally obliged to do so. Tables 5.3 and
5.4 show how they responded to the questions concerning whether
they had a legal or moral obligation to register bad behaviour or
attitudes with the social welfare committee or the social worker.
While hardly anybody thought they were legally or morally obliged
to report bad behaviour or attitudes to the committee, eight thought
they were legally obliged to register bad behaviour with the social
worker, and 14 felt under a moral obligation to do so.

Moreover in meetings with the social worker only nine contact
workers (eight from Karlskoga) claimed that clients were always
present and only 11 said they told the client everything that went on at
such meetings. In contacts with the social worker generally
(including telephone conversations for example) 12 admitted to
reporting examples of bad behaviour and 10 examples of bad
attitudes. Asked if they would report examples of children being
badly treated, or situations where they thought a child's health was in
danger, to the social worker, 22 said they would.

Table 5.2 Time spent with the
client each month by the contact
worker (excluding time spent by
contact families looking after
children for weekends)

less than one hour	1
1 hour	5
2-5 hours	8
6-10 hours	3
11-15 hours	2
16-20 hours	1
21-25 hours	3
Total contact workers	23

88

Preventative measures: support or control?

Table 5.3 Whether contact workers felt legally or morally obliged to register clients' bad behaviour or attitudes with the social welfare committee

| | Legally obliged | | Morally obliged | |
	bad behaviour	bad attitudes	bad behaviour	bad attitudes
yes	2	0	3	0
no	16	19	16	19
don't know	4	3	3	3
not applicable	1	1	1	1
Total contact workers	23	23	23	23

If we distinguish between CPs and CFs on the one hand or ex-övervakare and non-övervakare on the other, we find that both CPs and ex-övervakare are more likely to report a client's bad behaviour to the social worker, than CFs and non-övervakare. It is difficult to say however whether this is caused by the more problem-orientated work of the CPs or by the fact that so many of the CPs in the sample were ex-övervakare.

What does all this prove? It shows that while CPs and CFs saw themselves as loyal primarily to the clients and knew that they were not expected to write reports about them, over a third of them thought they had a *legal* obligation to report bad behaviour in general and many of them had in fact done so. Whether or not they were justified in doing so is neither here nor there. By their very existence they would seem to be potentially as much agents of social control as the old övervakare and even social workers themselves. They were appointed by the local authority and obviously had the opportunity to see more of what went on in a client's home than a social worker

Table 5.4 Whether contact workers felt legally or morally obliged to register clients' bad behaviour with the social worker

| | Legally obliged | | Morally obliged | |
	bad behaviour	bad attitudes	bad behaviour	bad attitudes
yes	8	2	14	4
no	9	17	7	17
don't know	6	4	2	2
Total contact workers	23	23	23	23

possibly had. They had regular access to social workers; the client was not always present nor were clients told everything that went on between the contact worker and the social worker; they felt legally obliged to report and often did report examples of bad behaviour. Legally and formally their function is not a controlling one, but informally and in fact, they cannot help but add to the surveillance of the more deprived. It will now be interesting to see whether clients experienced CPs and CFs as controlling.

The client's experience

Generally speaking there would seem to be a reasonable measure of agreement between contact workers and clients. Only one client claimed that the appointment of a CP was obligatory and all but three thought that such an appointment was the best way to help them. Fifteen of the 19 clients considered that contact work with them had been successful or very successful and only one thought it had not been at all successful. Only two claimed that it had achieved nothing. There were disagreements however.

When asked, for example, whether clients were present when contact workers met with social workers two-thirds of the contact workers said that this was always or often the case, while only one-fifth of the clients said it was (see Table 5.5). It is difficult to know how to interpret this but it certainly suggests that clients believed that contact workers and social workers met without them. Yet only four of them believed that examples of bad behaviour were reported. As stated above, CPs and CFs, in fact, reported bad behaviour in 12 cases and bad attitudes in 10. Only one client thought that contact workers wrote reports on them or were obliged to do so, but asked whether they thought that confidential information was given to the social worker seven said they did not know. That hardly suggests a high degree of certainty.

Whereas 96 per cent of the contact workers thought they ought to report to the social worker where they suspected a child was being badly treated, only 58 per cent of the clients agreed. Four (21 per cent) said no, they should not, while 3 (16 per cent) said they did not know. Much of this is a matter of degree but it does appear that a substantial number of clients did not have the same view of the situation as the contact worker; and some had a false impression of what was going on. This matter of degree came across too when the 5-point rankings of certain statements were compared for all respondents (see Table 5.6). Firstly it is clear that clients agreed strongly with both contact

Table 5.5 Whether the client was present when the
contact worker and the social worker met

	contact workers' responses	clients' responses
always	9	2
often	7	2
sometimes	2	5
never	1	7
they do not meet	—	2
no answer	4	1
Total	23	19

workers and social workers that the former were a support for the
client and that the work was inappropriate for social workers (many
clients said they were happier relating to an ordinary person rather
than somebody in authority). But it is also clear that clients generally
came closer to agreeing with the statements implying control (1 and
2) than contact workers or social workers.

Nothing better illustrates the ambiguous role of the clients'
situation than their responses to the question which gave them an
opportunity to say whether they preferred their present contact
worker, would like a different one or none at all. Sixteen preferred the
one they already had, which certainly suggests that whatever the

Table 5.6 Strength of agreement with five statements (the average scores
should be compared with a five-point scale whether STRONGLY AGREE =
1, AGREE = 2, NEITHER AGREE NOR DISAGREE = 3, DISAGREE = 4,
STRONGLY DISAGREE = 5)

	clients	contact workers	social workers
A contact person is an agent for the social worker	3.6	4.3	4.3
Contact work is an effective way to control clients	2.9	3.8	3.9
A contact person is, above all, a support for the client	1.5	1.4	1.4
Contact work ought to be carried out by social workers	4.1	3.9	4.1
Contact work is too stressful	4.6	4.3	3.4

element of control, their supportive role was appreciated. But in the three cases where the client had said they wanted other CPs or CFs or none at all, the social worker had refused or been uncooperative.

In conclusion, it cannot be said that clients experienced contact workers as a direct and oppressive form of control. Nevertheless, it is also clear that on the one hand clients were more likely to sense the potential for control where the other parties did not, yet on the other hand they seemed to be unaware at times of the degree of surveillance that existed in reality.

Social workers

As explained above, some of the social workers had responsibility for more than one case. Where cases are considered, the total possible responses will be 21; but where it is the individual views of the social workers that are being considered the total will be 14. It should also be made clear that many of the social workers had taken over cases from colleagues and were not as familiar with these as they were with cases for which they had been responsible from the outset.

Of the 14 social workers, all said that there was a difference between contact workers and övervakare and all but one described the difference accurately. Three thought there was a legal obligation for contact workers to register bad behaviour with the social worker and two with the welfare committee. If this is generally true, then a small minority of Swedish social workers have yet to grasp that there has been a change of policy. Moreover six considered that contact workers were morally obliged to register examples of bad behaviour with them.

Whereas only one client and one CP had described the contact work that had gone on as unsuccessful, social workers described six out of the 21 cases as unsuccessful.

Social workers tended to confirm the contact workers' impression of the number of cases where meetings between them also included the clients. In 18 of the 21 cases they also claimed that clients were told much or everything of what passed between them and contact workers. But they did not feel it necessary to tell contact workers everything about the clients. As the official guidelines suggested they were selective. And while all of them said that contact workers did not write reports, and that they were not obliged to do so, they confirmed that in many cases contact workers did inform them of examples of bad behaviour and attitudes.

Social workers then, confirm the impression conveyed by the

contact workers. A shift in policy has taken place; contact workers are indeed a support for the client; but the role inevitably involves a degree of surveillance and a link with the övervakare past.

Discussion

It is relevant to a discussion of the role of contact workers to consider a special characteristic of social work in Sweden. It is to social workers that people come when they need social bidrag (SB). This has both advantages and disadvantages. The advantage claimed is that social workers are able to advise clients on their entitlement to a whole range of benefits, and where they discover that the problems a client has are not simply financial, they are able to offer other kinds of assistance and treatment. The support of a contact worker is but one example. The disadvantages are firstly, that as a consequence of dispensing SB, both clients and social workers suffer a degree of stigmatisation. Clients may feel that in applying for money they are going to have their lives and problems investigated. Certainly, some Swedish social workers see it as their responsibility to discover what other problems people have. As a consequence, social workers themselves are often seen as interfering and are regarded with distrust. Secondly, with the increase in recent years of applications for SB, social workers often do not have the time to devote themselves to other social work activities, as they are so busy processing SB claims.

In Chapter 3, the proposal by the Commission to link the administration of SB with social insurance (SOFT) and the experiment in re-organisation in one district of Stockholm, were attempts to deal with this problem. The south district of Karlskoga had solved the dilemma by assigning some social workers to SB claims for nine months at a time and then giving them two years of traditional social work tasks, but in the rest of Karlskoga and in Vivalla-Lundby, social workers had the difficulty of coping with SB applications as well as their case-work.

The implications for contact work are not clear but there would seem to be two. One is that social workers may be tempted to use contact workers where they simply do not have the time to devote to clients. The other is that social workers may not have the time to adequately supervise what contact workers are doing. And when, in addition, it is considered that neither of the two local authorities was able to provide any kind of induction course or follow-up group work for contact workers, and that there were inadequate resources for recruitment, it is not surprising that this survey has revealed a certain amount of ambiguity surrounding the contact workers' role.

It is clear, however, that in many cases the contact policy is working remarkably well. This often came across most strongly in discussions with clients and contact workers after the formal interview. One father had been left some years previously by his wife. He had to bring up the children on his own and had real problems with his daughter who thought, wrongly, that he was preventing her from seeing her mother. A friend at work was an övervakare and the father asked social services if she could become a CP for his daughter. The relationship had worked very well and father and daughter now got on much better. He felt that the CP was a real friend and support.

Another client, whose husband had left her, had had the support of a CP for some years. She had found the task of bringing up her children very hard and felt isolated where she lived. She had been able to depend on her CP when all sorts of problems arose and currently, the eldest son, with whom she was having a difficult time, was actually living in the CP's house. The CP was an indispensable boon and never met with the social worker without the client being present.

A woman whose finances had always been managed either by her parents or by her husband, who had left her, found herself with enormous money problems. When she went to social services for SB, she found them very helpful. They suggested a CP who could help her manage her affairs. She now felt confident about managing money on her own.

Other single parents found the relief offered by CFs invaluable and had come to regard the families as real friends. There were other cases, however, where the client was not so happy. One nervous young mother obviously felt that the CF was a real imposition. The suggestion of a CF had come from one of the assistants at her child's nursery and that same person had put herself forward for the job. The client seemed too weak and powerless to resist the idea.

In another interview the client, a mother, resented the questions. She felt that they were irrelevant since they implied she was a social problem whereas she had only sought a CF to help look after her daughter one weekend in the month. The CF, on the other hand, thought of her as an alcoholic and resented the fact that she had not been forewarned about the client's problem. She complained that social services had failed to give her adequate support, training or guidance.

One CP said that a particular client, who had refused to be interviewed, had not wanted a CP but that the social worker had insisted. In a similar case, a young woman certainly saw the CP as a controlling agent and not much of a support and had asked for a CF instead. This request, she claimed, had been rejected.

THE MEANING OF CONTROL

It would perhaps be useful at this point to examine a little more closely this distinction between support and control. In public debate and policy conflicts there is always the danger that issues become artificially polarised. In much of the literature and many of the arguments looked at in previous chapters clear-cut distinctions have been made by opposing groups. In the same way the advocacy of contact workers as opposed to övervakare became very much bound up with the debate concerning compulsion in the social services generally. But when we actually look at what is happening between contact workers, social workers and their clients there are many grey areas. It is therefore important to make some distinctions about what we mean by control.

In one sense the appointment of a contact worker does automatically imply surveillance and control. But not necessarily more so than that exercised by a friend or relative. Indeed, in one of the cases cited above, it was a lesbian co-habitee who reported a mother's ill-treatment of her child to social services. It could have been her CP but would such an act of control make either of them agents of social control like social workers, probation officers and övervakare? The latter may be appointed by the state to keep an eye on people's behaviour and report accordingly, but contact workers are appointed as a resource for the client and not the state or the local authority. Their obligation to report misbehaviour and neglect is no greater than that of an ordinary member of the public. Inevitably, however,they will find themselves involved in acts of control. That is both acceptable and understandable.

While it is not the purpose of this study to make recommendations on how the Swedes might change their system, the voluntary principle that the reformers want to strengthen might be aided by a strengthening of the voluntary sector itself. To begin with it might make sense to use övervakare for compulsory supervision and contact workers for voluntary support, rather than rely on a policy that uses one or the other exclusively. In consequence it would make sense to have separate associations for both groups, rather than the joint association that exists at present. But more significantly, perhaps, the separate associations could be given the autonomy to organise and finance the work of övervakare and contact workers, independently of the local authorities. If contact workers are intended to be a resource for the client, there should be no need for them to have to meet and communicate with social workers at all. The potential for control, beyond that of any ordinary citizen, only arises because the authorities persist in maintaining strong links with contact workers. The weaker these links become, the more independent a contact worker can be and be seen to be. A similar system operates in the UK with Homestart, a voluntary organisation, which provides help to families with young children. The volunteer is not appointed or paid by social services and has no obligation to liaise with any state agencies. The independence of the voluntary organisation means that those helped can in no way feel that the helper is acting in a supervisory capacity.[1]

The real danger in Sweden is that contact workers could become more explicitly used by the authorities as agents of control and in consequence come to see themselves and be seen by the clients in this way. This is illustrated by some of the responses to the survey but more seriously by a change in the law in 1985.

INTERMEDIATE FORCE

In 1984, the Minister for Health and Social Affairs, Girtrud Sigurdsen, proposed a change in the law relating to the compulsory care of young people (LVU). The measure, which came to be known as 'mellan-tvång' – intermediate force – was incorporated into the legislation a year later and was retained in the more drastic revisions of the law mentioned in the previous chapter. It involved the introduction of compulsory measures to deal with young drug addicts, alcoholics and delinquents which fell between the voluntary measures of SoL and the compulsory care of LVU – hence the term 'intermediate force'. In particular it enabled social services to force a young person to have regular contact with a CP and to participate in open forms of treatment provided by social services.

Sigurdsen justified this measure on the basis of statistics which indicated rising problems among young people between 1981 and 1982. When the proposal went out on remiss, it revived the battle over compulsion that had been waged throughout the 1970s. The

Commission that had been set up to review the social services legislation was against the proposal, although it subsequently had to incorporate it into its own proposals. It was backed by the Swedish Association of Kommuns, which attacked the measure as a return to the old thumbscrew philosophy with its compulsory övervakare (Svenska kommunförbundet 1984). It blamed the worsening economic situation and the cuts in social services for the introduction of a panic measure.

The major trade union federations, LO and TCO, were against it, as were the local authorities representing the three major cities of Stockholm, Gothenburg and Malmö, and Socialstyrelsen, and client organisations such as RFHL and Verdandi. For the measure, were the administrative boards that dealt with crime and the police, organisations representing the judiciary and public prosecutors, RNS and FMN. The line-up was almost identical to that of the 1970s debate on compulsion with the SAP split down the middle (*Narkotikafrågan* 31 (1985). The right wing representatives of the Swedish Association of Kommuns dissented from the majority report and came out for intermediate force saying that social workers needed stronger measures to deal with the problems they faced. When it came to a vote in the Riksdag the SAP toed the government line after an appeal for unity by the then Prime Minister, Olof Palme. The three bourgeois parties also supported the government. The communist party, VPK, voted against it together with a mere five social democrats with five others abstaining (Riksdag 1985).

CONCLUSION

The movement away from a reliance on a compulsory approach towards a more voluntary one, in Swedish social services, is reflected in the use of preventative measures. Instead of the old controls of warnings, instructions and övervakare, contact persons and families are used as a form of support. The survey carried out in two local authority areas suggests that this change has been largely successful in embodying the intentions of the legislation and the official guidelines. However, in a minority of cases there did seem to be evidence of control, compulsion and misunderstanding. Some of this could easily be put right by a greater emphasis upon training and clearer supervision at the local level, the lack of which, in both authorities, was put down to insufficient resources and a lack of time.

Contact workers need to be more aware of what their tasks and responsibilities are and the principles on which they are based. Present cuts in social services will do nothing to help the situation, which is unfortunate, because contact workers do seem to be a cheap and effective preventative measure, valued by clients and social workers alike.

But no amount of formal training will prevent the deliberate abuse by some individuals, of what is supposed to be a voluntary and supportive measure. Clients are vulnerable and can easily be manipulated to accept a situation against their real wishes. Such manipulation is not very different from the compulsion that SoL was seeking to avoid. The temptation to manipulate the intentions of SoL in general, and preventative measures in particular, must be very great especially for those who feel strongly about alcohol and drug-abuse. And the survey showed that a high proportion of the clients had a drug or alcohol problem.

Nor has the situation been helped, at a national level, by the introduction of 'intermediate force'. This measure was introduced to take a tougher line with young people suspected of having an alcohol or a drug problem, and was supported by those individuals and organisations who feel strongly about drug and alcohol-abuse. But the role of some CPs is now indistinguishable from that of övervakare. Such a blurring of what was an important distinction will not help to persuade clients that contact workers are intended to be a support for them rather than an extension of social services' control apparatus.

While this case study has shown that the extent to which social services seek to control their clients through preventative measures is more potential than real, the following case study demonstrates that the potentially and reality of control through the administration of social assistance is much greater.

NOTE

1. These comments are based upon a discussion I had with a Homestart Organiser in Loughborough, to whom I explained how contact work was organised in Sweden.

CHAPTER SIX
The right to social assistance

INTRODUCTION

British social policy is obsessed with 'scrounging' or the abuse of social security. The press, periodically goes in for bouts of scrounger-bashing. Sensational and lurid stories appear about social assistance claimants making false and multiple claims. They are reported as having jobs on the side and leading luxurious lives on the Costa Del Sol. Police raids are made on single homeless men, social security officials spy on the private lives of single parents who are reputed to be co-habiting, and the unemployed are accused of being work-shy. Some abuse obviously exists as an inevitable consequence of our having created a system in which such large numbers of people are dependent upon means-tested benefits. Much of it is exaggerated in order to whip up public hostility towards welfare claimants.

In my first visit to Sweden in 1982 the impression gained was that the abuse of social assistance there was a non-issue. Interviews with politicians, officials and social workers suggested that the problem existed but was regarded as very minor indeed.

> Social workers are responsible for the administration of social assistance and make it their job to advise on welfare rights at the same time. There is no attempt to conceal from claimants what rights they have to benefits; on the contrary, it would almost seem as if the system operates to ensure that maximum claims are made. (Gould 1984a: p. 17)

One group of social workers said that they would not dream of providing a client with second-hand furniture – it had to be new. Application forms for social assistance seemed to be short and simple. In short, claimants had a right to social assistance which gave them a good standard of living.

While all of this is no doubt true, subsequent investigations have suggested that the Swedes have another obsession which creates problems for claimants. Put briefly it is a preoccupation with self-improvement which manifests itself in a number of ways not least of which is the concern shown about the way in which people damage themselves through the consumption of alcohol and drugs. This has already been alluded to earlier in the book and will be dealt with in more detail in the next chapter, but it is mentioned now because there is a concern in Sweden about people becoming dependent upon social assistance and it is linked directly and indirectly with attitudes towards dependence upon alcohol and drugs. Claimants have to be weened from such dependencies but the dispute is about how this can best be achieved.

This case study is centred around the introduction of a new approach to the administration of social assistance by a group of social workers based in the Stockholm suburb of Alby. But before describing that approach and the repercussions that followed, it is necessary to consider what the 1982 Social Services Act (SoL) had to say about social assistance and the advice Socialstyrelsen gave to kommuns about the principles that should guide its administration. The chapter concludes by suggesting that although the Alby dispute was about whether social workers should take a hard or a soft line with social assistance claimants, it was not primarily a dispute between the political right and the political left. Most of those who engaged in the public debate about Alby were socialists. It is therefore more accurate to suggest that the dispute was between different factions of the left – one tending towards a more authoritarian approach, the other towards a more libertarian one. In conclusion it is suggested that there are a number of reasons for linking the Alby dispute with the position adopted by individuals and groups engaged in the politics of drug and alcohol abuse.

SOCIAL ASSISTANCE IN THE 1980s

There is little doubt that social assistance in Sweden is administered more efficiently and generously than in England. This is partly a consequence of having a strong economy and full employment, but partly because the welfare system is so organised as to diminish the necessity for people to depend on assistance. Pensioners, the unemployed, and those who are sick have high income replacement levels through social insurance; and the active labour market policy ensures that there are many schemes and accompanying allowances which make it unnecessary for many others to claim SB (Greve 1978, Wilson 1979). Nevertheless, the system does have problems and faults. Economic problems and welfare cuts have made Swedes more cost conscious, while growing unemployment, even if still low by European standards, has helped to swell the numbers of those on SB, as have problems concerning immigrants and single parent families. Social workers have found that more and more of their time is spent processing claims and less on case work and there has been discussion about the possibility of linking SB with social insurance administration as happens in England. For, in spite of the reform of social services in 1982, the administration of social assistance in Sweden remains a matter for local kommuns and social workers – a responsibility jealously guarded by some.

Section 6 of the 1982 Social Services Act states that:

> The individual is entitled to assistance from the social welfare committee towards his livelihood and other aspects of living if his needs cannot be provided in any other way. The assistance must assure the individual of a reasonable level of living. The assistance must be designed in such a way as to strengthen the independent living resources of the individual.
> (Ministry of Health and Social Affairs 1981)

This is developed further in the advice given to local authorities by Socialstyrelsen (Socialstyrelsen 1981). Social services should aim to give those seeking help, economic and social security, equality of living conditions and the opportiunity to play a citizen's full part in the life of society. Even those working part-time or on low incomes have a right to claim, to bring their incomes up to local SB levels. However the advice also stresses that assistance should not be without conditions. Individuals are responsible for their own lives and it is not the job of a local authority to encourage dependence on state benefits. The point is to strengthen and complement individuals' own resources so that they can eventually manage without assistance and lead independent lives. But this should not mean forcing individuals to accept certain forms of treatment or types of measure, or imposing social workers' own values on the client. Those seeking help should be offered a full range of measures and helped to choose what is most appropriate to their own values and situation. The process should be an active cooperation between social services and the client, with the ultimate aim of rehabilitation and independence. Social workers can influence and guide but not direct and force.

Local authorities have then the 'ultimate responsibility' to help claimants and claimants have a clear responsibility to help themselves. But if individuals refuse care or treatment or will not seek work, the local authority still has the responsibility to satisfy their need. 'One must be very restrictive with measures that can be seen as an interference with a person's integrity' (Ibid.: p. 19). Force can never be a part of measures under the social services law. If force is necessary then other, more appropriate legislation must be used.

As with the policy on contact persons, the emphasis in the new legislation is on assistance agreed to voluntarily, and against the use of force and compulsion. But as with 'voluntary' confessions in police interrogations, the word can have a number of interpretations yet remain true to its meaning. Even in the advice outlined above it is suggested that a social worker can legitimately 'influence' a client. If influence, why not persuasion? And if persuasion does not work, is pressure justified? Moreover, the concept of 'ultimate responsibility' by some social workers is taken to mean that if people come to them with problems they have an obligation to help them. A client may simply come asking for SB, but after a while the social worker is bound to enquire about the problems that are leading to a dependence on state help. After all the legislation itself says that one must aim to rehabilitate the individual and wean the client off an addiction to SB.

If the client is an alcoholic, then at the very least, various forms of treatment ought to be discussed; if the client has behaviour problems then some therapy might be in order; the single parent could be encouraged to have a CP or CF (see Chapter 5), or leave the child at a day nursery and seek employment; the work-shy should be encouraged to look for work even if that is difficult, since they might in the end lose the habit of work.

When situations such as these arise in the English situation they are dealt with by two different sets of people – the social security officer, dealing with money, and the social worker dealing with other forms of help. In Sweden it is the social worker who, together with the client, must make the decisions. The social worker must play an active, not a passive part. Local authorities, according to the law, have 'ultimate responsibility' (Ministry of Health and Social Affairs 1981). People should be helped to become independent, yet this must be done voluntarily. Is it any wonder that social workers find their role difficult, or that clients who don't want to help themselves or who find themselves disagreeing about the appropriate form of help, finish up resenting interference by social workers?

The dilemma is created by having to dispense SB on the one hand

and forms of treatment, care and therapy on the other; by having to help people who cannot help themselves in such a way that they can help themselves. While the legislators and Socialstyrelsen may have felt that such dilemmas should be resolved in a fairly liberal way others have taken a different line.

THE WORKING PARTY ON SOCIALBIDRAG

Soon after the 1982 reforms were enacted, the numbers of people receiving SB began to increase as did the cost to local authorities. Public concern led to much speculation about the reasons for this. Two of the theories put forward, in explanation, were that the increases were due to the 1982 reforms and the fact that a new category of people had begun to benefit. The term 'the new poor' was used to describe the allegation that house-owners, full-time workers and people on average incomes were benefiting from SB. Girtrud Sigurdsen, the Minister for Social Affairs, reacted sharply to this and set up a working party to investigate the problem. In its preliminary report (Socialdepartementet 1986) it looked at the facts and asked local authorities for their explanations.

The report showed that between 1981 and 1985 the numbers of people (adults and children) benefiting from SB increased from 343,000 to 534,000; the number of households from 178,000 to 294,000; while the cost to local authorities doubled to SKR 3358 million (£330 million). Whereas in 1875 4.4 per cent of the population had been given needs-tested social assistance, and in 1975 5.1 per cent, in 1984 the figure was 6.1 per cent. In the UK, the comparable percentage of the population living on supplementary benefit is over 16 per cent (Wicks 1987), but the Swedish figures still gave cause for concern. How, the working party asked, could this come about when society already had a comprehensive welfare state. Part of the explanation, it suggested, was that poverty was relative and that as standards rose so did new needs. But it rejected any notion that a category of 'new poor' had come into being. On the contrary, many claimants came from the same categories, with the exception of the elderly, as in the past – the unemployed, the sick and those thrown onto the scrap-heap by structural changes in the economy (Socialdepartementet 1986: part 1, ch. 1).

Although unemployment was still low by international comparisons, it had risen from 2 per cent in 1980 to 3.8 per cent in 1983. Moreover a quarter of the work-force was in part-time work. Eighty per cent of households on SB were single adults with and without children. Single men were the biggest group here while single women without children had doubled. Even with SB the incomes of such people were 20 per cent below comparable groups. Sixty per cent of SB claimants in one year had been on SB the year before and many of them had previously had to rely on sickness benefit. Sixty per cent were under the age of 30 and as a proportion of all recipients the young were increasing. Less than 2 per cent of those over 65 claimed SB. Most SB claimants lived in rented property and families with two parents, or large numbers of children, had declined as a proportion of all beneficiaries (Ibid.).

When different local authorities were compared it was clear that the larger ones in the big cities had a higher proportion of SB beneficiaries but it was also clear that many of these had greater employment opportunities than many smaller towns. Unemployment was then only part of the explanation of growing SB dependence. When local authorities were asked for their explanations, they confirmed that unemployment, particularly among young people, was a major factor. Students and other young, single people formed an increasing proportion of claimants. Other categories were more diffuse. Single people often had other problems. They might be physically or mentally sick and/or have an alcohol or drug problem. Limited job opportunities hit members of this group particularly hard. In Kristianstad only 7 per cent of SB claimants had an alcohol or a drug problem; in Örebro 10 per cent; in Solna it was estimated at 12 per cent; while in Lund the figure was put at about a third. In Helsingborg, the local authority examined a large number of long-term dependants (those in receipt of SB for more than nine months) and concluded that the biggest single category, 42 per cent had an alcohol or a drug problem. Sundsvall reported a figure of half all long-term beneficiaries on drugs. For single men this figure rose to two-thirds (Ibid., part 2, ch. 1).

One other factor associated with the increases in SB claimants was that of refugees and immigrants from outside the Nordic area. While some of the local authorities reported around 10 per cent of all households in this group, in Stockholm it was claimed that it accounted for 40 per cent of the actual growth in numbers (Ibid., part 2, ch. 1). Given that the capital city is also reputed to have a large drugs problem as well, it is not surprising that a major dispute about the administration of social assistance arose in one of its suburbs.

ALBY

Alby is one of those modern suburbs built in the 1960s and 70s on the outskirts of Stockholm, to help solve the housing problem and to cope with the increased labour migration which was the result of economic expansion. By the 1980s, many of them had a high proportion of immigrant workers and their families and some, like Alby and Rinkeby, had more than their fair share of unemployment, social problems and SB beneficiaries. To many better-off Swedes, these estates had a reputation of being problem areas in which it was undesirable to live. The areas then began to experience the kind of downward spiral of deprivation all too familiar to those who know something of the sink estates of Britain.

To the British eye these suburbs still have a long way to go before the deprivation becomes as visible as in the UK (although it must be admitted that over a period of a few months during 1986 and 1987, many of them including Alby, suddenly and inexplicably became festooned with the most grotesque graffiti). The visitor who travels by Tunnelban (Stockholm's underground railway) to these suburban estates emerges into a shopping precinct which also contains the principal services and offices. Everything looks modern, clean and spacious if somewhat impersonal. As you wander around it soon becomes clear that the whole suburb has been planned with a lot of forethought. While some of the accommodation consists of high-rise blocks, there is much low-level housing as well. The building and design is of a high quality and there is little evidence of vandalism. The separation of roads (for cars) from paths (for pedestrians and cyclists) is arranged in a way that ensures maximum accessibility and maximum safety. Children can play among the trees and bushes and in the solidly designed play areas with little fear of meeting with traffic. Everywhere there is evidence of planners paying a great deal of attention to people's living needs.

Social services in Alby are administered from an area office of the larger Botkyrka Kommun. One of the social workers who joined the office when it first opened in 1975 described it as having long waiting times for appointments, too few employees and a high staff turnover (Sundelin 1985). Addicts and alcoholics were simply given money since there was so little time for anything else. During the 1970s, the number of claimants had grown but the resources to deal with them had not kept pace. Morale was very low.

Influenced by Tony Manocchio, an American consultant, a new intake team, from 1980, began to develop what subsequently became

known as the 'responsibility model'. The basic idea seemed to be that
social workers, to become effective, had to prevent themselves from
becoming overwhelmed by their clients' problems. Instead of taking
the view that clients were the weak and incapable victims of economic
and social forces who needed constant support, social workers should
aim to develop clients' resources – both material and personal – and
networks so that they could manage their own affairs. Tasks which
before social workers had done for clients, clients would now do for
themselves. Since it was the intake team that met with new applicants
for assistance and decided whether to turn people away, deal with
them on the spot or refer them to the child care team or the social
assistance/drug and alcohol-abuse team (an interesting combination
of tasks in itself), the way in which they interpreted their role was
rather crucial both for clients and the functioning of the rest of the
department. As far as the intake team and their social services
colleagues were concerned the new approach was much more
rewarding and successful and morale increased. Social workers felt
they were achieving something positive rather than simply mopping
up problems as they arose (Sundelin 1985). Unfortunately this view
was not shared by all their colleagues in other services nor all their
clients.

Socialstyrelsen investigates

A number of complaints in 1984, from clients and workers in other
agencies led Socialstyrelsen to investigate what was going on in Alby.
Early in 1985 a report was produced which alleged that those who
sought help from social services in Alby were humiliated and insulted
by social workers there (Socialstyrelsen 1985a). The evidence for this
was based upon conversation and interviews with some clients,
personnel from the employment office, probation service and the
immigrant bureau, a couple of interpreters and a teacher. The details
were made known to the press and sensationalised accounts in many
national newspapers followed. The social workers in Alby, the
District Council to which they were responsible and Botkyrka
Kommun were outraged. What ensued was a lively public and
professional debate in which the Alby team maintained that they had
been unjustifiably pilloried, while Socialstyrelsen continued to
collect and produce evidence in support of its case.

Socialstyrelsen produced a further report in April 1985 based on
additional evidence that had come to light (Socialstyrelsen 1985b).
The Kommun replied with a defence in May enlisting the help of

The right to social assistance

Svenska Kommunförbundet – the Swedish Association of Kommuns – (Botkyrka Kommun 1985) and Socialstyrelsen wrote a final report based upon social work records in July (Socialstyrelsen 1985c). Meanwhile individual clients registered complaints with the ombudsman, and Botkyrka Kommun registered a JK (judicial chancellor) complaint against Socialstyrelsen.

Far from being a local dispute, Alby became an ideological battleground for welfare bureaucrats and professionals, politicians and academics all over the country. Part of the dispute concerned the way in which Socialstyrelsen had gone about its investigation. This will be referred to later. But the ideological battle demonstrated that there was more than one way of interpreting the 1982 law and that advocates for both sides of the dispute could be found up and down the land.

The Allegations

Socialstyrelsen (what follows is based largely on Socialstyrelsen 1985c) was obviously convinced that the Alby social workers were acting in a way contrary to the letter and spirit of the 1982 Act which was supposed to be a new departure from previous legislation. The Act was based upon a fundamental respect for individuals, their rights, their independence and integrity. The old child-care, social assistance and temperance laws had contained elements of compulsion, coercion and punishment. The new, unified, law was based upon voluntary cooperation between social services and its clients. What was being said about Alby and the new methods being employed there, led Socialstyrelsen to believe that the law and the advice that it gave to local authorities was being openly flouted. However up-to-date the new methods were, they seemed to have the same effect as the old poor legislation.

Socialstyrelsen alleged that:

1. It was difficult for clients to get appointments. They were questioned on the telephone about why they wanted help and social workers decided there and then whether they had a right to assistance and whether they had other resources they could use. The effect was to discourage applications for help. People were being put off in their attempts to seek assistance. Moreover social workers were making judgements on too little information.
2. Some help-seekers tried to make appointments through their probation officers or officers from the immigrant bureau but social

107

workers were insisting that clients act for themselves. While this was not happening in all cases, the fact was that it was an individual's right to use a representative to act on her/his behalf.

3. There was a requirement that when an application for help was made by one partner in a marriage, both had to attend the interview. Since there were many instances where this could have a detrimental or embarrassing effect (e.g. in the case of a battered woman) and since such matters might be difficult to discuss in a telephone call requesting an appointment, it was both unnecessary and insensitive to insist on such a rule. While it might be necessary sometimes in order to check the validity of claims being made, there was no need for a general requirement.

4. People seeking assistance were often bombarded with questions about their personal circumstances in the manner of an interrogation. Their answers were treated with suspicion. The manner of the social workers was aggressive. Clients were asked to formulate their needs precisely and where they could not they were driven to distraction by their interrogators.

5. SB was not granted as a right but as something the client had to earn. The demands and conditions placed upon the client were difficult to meet. They were often formulated at too early a stage in the application for benefit. Some clients were expected to show evidence that they had made a number of job applications every day. Conditions were insisted upon which the labour market authorities themselves would not require. While it was right that an employable person should be at the disposal of the labour market, it was also right to see that people were given assistance in seeking, acquiring and keeping jobs. It was also suspected that alcoholics and drug addicts were being made to accept treatment as a condition of receiving SB. This was unjustified. If an individual had a right to SB, then the request should not be used as a means of fulfilling other social policy aims. Although the law stated that SB entitlement should not be without demands, it was important that social workers learn how to put these demands in a sensitive way. Individuals should be able to consider forms of treatment and help, and choose or reject them voluntarily. It was important to know how to handle the client with a rehabilitative aim in mind. How the individual reacted to and adapted to a demand was of fundamental importance. While social workers were entitled to make investigations relevant to an application for financial assistance it was wrong to try to find out if there were related social problems and circumstances immediately the first contact was made.

6. The use of techniques borrowed from psychotherapy was inappropriate in social services. Clients' words and statements were being played around with in a manner which was experienced as insulting. One client was subjected to a role-play performance by social workers who tried to demonstrate that an employer would find her manner unacceptable.

7. Another inappropriate method borrowed from the realms of therapy was the use of an observer. Many clients complained that while they were being interviewed by one social worker, another was looking on. Sometimes the observer said nothing or sat behind the client, giving a sense of unease, sometimes the observer discussed the client with the social worker while referring to the client in the third person. Although the local authority claimed that this method was helpful to both client and social worker, since the observer was able to provide an additional perspective, Socialstyrelsen considered it oppressive and unsuitable and far from being an impartial technique.

8. There was a poor relationship with other social agencies. The law required social services to cooperate with other authorities yet in Alby many of these complained that social services treated them badly.

In addition Socialstyrelsen claimed that clients were being kept waiting too long for appointments; were misinformed about their rights to benefits and rights of appeal; and were given benefits at levels too low for them to live on.

Throughout its report on the social workers' own case records, Socialstyrelsen frequently quoted the comments and views of three professors of social work in three Swedish universities, Stockholm, Gothenburg and Umeå, two heads of other social services departments and a psychiatrist, in support of its own case.

Socialstyrelsen's supporters

Among others who supported Socialstyrelsen in its criticism of Alby's social services, were the chairman of RFHL (National Association to help addicts) and the probation officers of Botkyrka Kommun. The former claimed that Alby was simply the tip of an iceberg and that the recession in the economy was making the poor vulnerable. In other words it was no coincidence that the responsibility model should become popular just at the same time as the number of people dependent on SB was increasing. And by suggesting that Alby was the tip of an iceberg, the chairman of RFHL was suggesting that such attitudes and practices were not confined to just one locality (Socionomen 1985).

The probation officers applauded Socialstyrelsen's report, saying that their own fears had now been confirmed. They had been told by those at Alby that criminal care clients could be treated no differently to anybody else. The new method put clients at a disadvantage, whereas the law had intended to make social services more accessible. The Alby method demanded that clients should analyse and solve their own problems and when their attempts to do so failed, they were greeted with cynicism. This was little more than bullying by the authorities. They agreed that people had to be motivated and circumstances investigated but this needed time and required more skill, will and imagination than was shown in Alby (Fornell 1985).

The case for the defence

The official Botkyrka Kommun reply, largely written by Mats Christiansson, the District Head of the Alby Office, is a careful and rather bland document (Botkyrka Kommun 1985). While it attacked Socialstyrelsen's methods and conclusions, it admitted that there might be faults that could be corrected and suggested at the end how this might be done, in a tone of conciliation. At all times the argument sought to show that however different the Alby approach, it was simply an alternative way of implementing both the law and the general advice given by Socialstyrelsen.

The aim of the method was to help the clients see that there were alternative solutions to their problems. It sought to elicit the knowledge and resources of clients and to reveal to them that they had greater potential than they had thought. This often required a thorough and professional investigation into clients' problems. Social workers tried to get clients to state as clearly as possible what it was that they wanted and why it was that they thought they could not solve their problems other than by coming to social services. Earlier attempts to solve the problems were discussed and new ways of seeing the problems were explored. Then attempts were made to discover the long-term wishes of clients. After this the client's help in formulating alternative solutions was sought. The way was then clear for client and social worker together to formulate a plan of action for the future, with clear, concrete and realisable goals. The law and Socialstyrelsen's advice said that assistance was not to be given free of conditions and demands, and that people were to be helped to lead an independent life. The Alby method aimed to do just that.

Socialstyrelsen's initial report was based upon nine cases out of the 2000 subjects that the office had to deal with over the previous two years. Out of that number there were bound to be people who felt that their wishes had not been met, and who were aggrieved about the decisions that had been made. Yet, in 1984 there had only been 15 appeals to the County Court by clients and in only one of these had the judgement of the Department been reversed.

Contrary to what was said by Socialstyrelsen, waiting times for appointments were no longer than in other offices – one to two weeks – and there were clear arrangements for dealing with emergency cases. Representatives for clients could arrange appointments, but it was important to meet clients alone to sort out their personal problems. Where there were language difficulties, there was no problem about the use of interpreters. As for the presence of an observer, that enabled a social worker to enlist the help of a colleague on the spot. The alternative would be for the social worker to discuss difficult problems with colleagues behind the client's back. Since clients often had someone with them to cope with the interview, where was the difference when a social worker needed the support of a colleague? The report complained that clients were sometimes encouraged to see if they could borrow money from friends, relatives, neighbours or the bank, yet in the general advice given to local authorities they were asked to do just that. You could not expect to go into people's problems and resources and in every case be obliging and agree with them. People were bound to go away feeling depressed or dissatisfied at times. Differences and conflict were inevitable in some cases. While a lot of energy went into avoiding this and there might be grounds for making a greater attempt, conflict could not be completely avoided.

The Kommun had enlisted the independent help of Kommun-förbundet to examine the accounts of clients quoted by Socialstyrelsen, and to find out whether the degree of cooperation between social services and other agencies was as bad as had been alleged. Botkyrka's interpretation of Kommunförbundet's report was that it showed that far from there being unanimous opposition, many agencies strongly supported the Alby office and none were wholly negative in their criticisms. It was not surprising that agencies should disagree about how clients should be treated or about the appropriateness of different sets of demands or treatment. A resource-oriented agency such as social services, operating with a structured approach, was bound to differ with an agency which was not resource-oriented and had an unstructured approach. Moreover many of the client accounts were unreliable, factually incorrect and quoted out of context. It was felt that Socialstyrelsen's reliance upon client accounts to the exclusion of the views of social workers was to be deplored. More generally it was felt that all social work methods needed systematic evaluation, not just Alby's. Alby had found its previous practices ineffective and that was why they had begun to change five years previously. New methods needed time to be properly developed and evaluated and should not be judged hastily.

While Botkyrka rejected much of Socialstyrelsen's report, it did accept the need for further research into Alby's methods; the need for members of the welfare committee and the social services department to become more accessible and the need for a seminar in which other agencies and social services could discuss the issue of cooperation.

Comments by the Alby social workers

Generally speaking, the interviews that Alby's social workers gave to various journals tended to agree with the argument above but did also illustrate the greater harshness of the Alby approach in a way that the Botkyrka report did not. Christiansson himself was quoted as saying that if the department had a rule that spouses should present themselves together at interviews then there could not be exceptions, although his report claims there could. Another social worker criticised the social work assistant who had complained about the unfriendly nature of interviews with clients, by saying that it was not her job to get mixed up with the client but to keep a professional distance from the problem. The characteristic of friends was that you chose them. This was confirmed by a male colleague who said that clients did not come to social workers to have a relationship (Sundelin 1985).

In another interview, the same social worker admitted that compared with critics in other social services departments, Alby did impose more demands and carry out more investigations. In the past, when clients who had been told to bring certain papers with them, failed to do so, social workers would ring round for the information, whereas now they would send them home to get them (Kristensson and Landahl 1985). Where clients discontinued a form of treatment and came back for further help, the answer would be that now they would get the help they needed as opposed to the help they wanted. Deductions would be made to their SB entitlement where for example a client claimed SB on return from a holiday in Majorca. But deductions were always well justified. They would investigate the existence of bills and arrears and did examine whether people's networks and resources could be used for loans rather than pay out SB (Persson 1985b).

At a debate on the responsibility model, held at ABF (the workers' education association) in Stockholm, Björn Löfholm, the leader of the intake team, insisted that the team accepted and worked to the letter of the new law. The law said that claimants should be helped with more than just money; that they should be helped to be responsible for their own situation and to develop their own resources; that help should not be given without conditions. He claimed that it was precisely because the Alby social workers respected people's independence and integrity that they placed demands on them and helped them to change their situation. He used the example of alcohol and drug abuse to show that by helping people to end their addiction, they were being helped to be independent and went on to quote, not the actual legislation but a preliminary report which had said that: 'The social welfare committee must always work positively to reach and help people who have an addiction problem *even if they themselves have not requested help from the committee*' (my italics) (SoU 1979/80; 44 p. 107). He added: 'This is to say that some attempt must be made to do something, even if someone only wants financial assistance' (Löfholm 1985: p. 2). Löfholm was clearly interpreting the paragraph as forcefully as possible and it is clear that it is open to a weak and a strong interpretation. The 'voluntary' interpretation would be that you offer an addict help but respect his right to refuse it. The 'compulsory' one would be that you help him whether he likes it or not. It would seem probable that Löfholm's interpretation, and that of his colleagues, would have leant towards the latter. His contribution to the debate concluded with the statement: 'The responsibility model has nothing to do with the new individualism or the principle, look after yourself and shit on the others. We have a legally-stated obligation to care and besides, that is the tradition of this country' (Ibid p. 3). It is clear from this statement that Löfholm was at pains to distance himself from the politics of the new right and he felt that he and his fellow workers were working in the best traditions of socialist temperance.

Earlier, in his contribution to the debate, Löfholm had also made it clear that he was opposed to attempts to separate the administration of SB from support and treatment. This can only have meant that he was not in favour of the SOFT reform. A similar stand was taken by Anders Sundelin in an article vindicating the Alby social workers, one year after the dispute blew up. In it he wrote:

Conflict and control in welfare policy

> SOFT ... aims to unify the payment of SB so that certain people are
> rejected by social work offices. The sick, young people independent of
> their parents, the unemployed, the low-paid, amongst others, shall
> receive payment solely through the post. Spokesmen, such as those from
> Socialstyrelsen, claim that social services will have to concentrate their
> work on those who most need personal assistance. This system would
> naturally go against the labour movement's traditional view of social
> assistance in which SB is regarded as a kind of help to self-help.
>
> (Expressen 1986b)

If one assumes that Sundelin, who wrote many articles in support of
the Alby social workers, was not simply expressing a personal
opinion, then one can conclude that, struggling to get out of the Alby
debate, was a socialist view of social policy that had little in common
with those other socialists who had fought throughout the 1970s to
liberalise Swedish social welfare.

Outside supporters

Although it would be impossible to gauge the exact strength of the
two camps in this dispute, it is important to note that a petition,
attacking Socialstyrelsen, was signed by 281 social workers, researchers
and lecturers throughout the country, in June 1985. A number of the
contributors to the debate in one of Sweden's professional social work
journals also took the side of their colleagues in Alby. One, who
worked for the same Kommun, though in another district, said that
she had always found the Alby social workers very approachable and
helpful and willing to discuss and explain their methods. She and a
colleague from Rinkeby expressed support for the view that clients
should be helped to help themselves (Mörner 1985).

Sten Åke-Stenberg, of the Institute for Social Research at
Stockholm University, attacked the conspiratorial nature of the
attack on Alby. He alleged that Socialstyrelsen had made up its mind
before the evidence was collected and was not interested in a dialogue.
He was suspicious of the reliability of the clients' accounts that were
quoted and thought it unwise anyway to base very much on clients'
accounts alone. He claimed that the press and academics had simply
jumped on Socialstyrelsen's bandwagon (Stenberg1985).

Lennart Grosin, of the University's Education Institute, attacked
the popular theory that social policies often failed because of the
prevailing structural inequalities in society. He thought that the Alby
workers showed that deprivation was far from being simply the result
of a mechanical process and that the deprived *could* help themselves.
What was needed was the kind of aggressive, welfare ideology that

The right to social assistance

was being formulated and implemented in Alby. To demonstrate that the Alby workers were not reactionary, he emphasised that it was part of their philosophy that full employment be restored and that people be given wages that they could live on (Grosin 1985). This reinforced the claim by Björn Löfholm that the responsibility model had more to do with the traditions of the labour movement than Social-styrelsen's philosophy (Sundelin 1985).

'Independent' investigations

The outcome of this dispute is not clear. Both sides were able to claim a sort of victory. The judicial chancellor (JK) said Socialstyrelsen had the right to act as it did since it had sufficient reason to be concerned and alarmed (*Narkotikafrågan* 1986 34). An assessor for länsstyrelsen (the county administrative board) backed the Alby office, on the basis of conversations with local politicians and administrators, an interview with Björn Löfholm and the opportunity to sit in on two meetings between clients and social workers. Hardly what one would call an inquiry! As for Botkyrka's claim that Alby had been exonerated by Kommunförbundet, it is difficult to agree with that interpretation. All that Kommunförbundet did was what Social-styrelsen should have done in the first place. It consulted a wider range of agencies to find out whether they felt that the Alby office could be described as cooperative or not; and set out the accusations made by clients alongside their case-records and the comments made by their social workers. But it did not analyse or pronounce on the material – it simply collected it (Svenska Kommunförbundet 1985a and b). All that can be deduced from the cases is that clients and social workers disagreed, while the agency accounts are merely evidence that the debate about compulsion had re-emerged, once again, in Alby. Indeed the agency responsible for the care of drug addicts said exactly that: 'The debate is a continuation of the 1970s discussion about individual freedom in relation to social compulsion' (Kommun-förbundet 1985a: p. 4). On the one hand there were agencies which took a 'voluntaristic' approach to their clients' problems and found that the Alby office was uncooperative, unsympathetic, unimaginative and inflexible. Their clients were insulted and their values rejected. These included the job centre (arbetsförmedlingen), probation, the immigrant bureau, and a school-teacher. On the other hand the drug care agency, the alcohol clinic, the police and the child psychiatrists thought the workers at Alby were models of cooperation. They intervened early and saw that people got the measures they needed to

Conflict and control in welfare policy

deal with their problems. The Kommunförbundet report showed that Alby had friends as well as enemies, but Kommunförbundet itself, while it disapproved of Socialstyrelsen's sloppy investigation, in no way indicated its support or otherwise for the responsibility model.

The General Director of Socialstyrelsen, who had not been supported by Girtrud Sigurdsen over the Alby affair, subsequently resigned, to take up another job, tired of her disputes with the Minister (*Expressen* 1986a). Those directly responsible for the investigation into Alby moved or were moved into other posts. The Alby workers claimed after a year had elapsed that they had not changed their methods, but the länsstyrelsen report showed that Botkyrka raised the level of socialbidrag; increased the numbers employed in all its districts; reduced the number of occasions when two social workers were present at interviews with clients; and improved the appointment system. The report also quoted the probation office and the immigrant bureau as noticing an improvement in attitudes at the Alby office after the media publicity (Länsstyrelsen 1986).

CONCLUSION

As with the debate about children in care it is very difficult to reach a judgement about issues which rest upon the individual treatment of a large number of cases. All those engaged in the debate were defending particular views or interests which an outside observer cannot easily pronounce upon. Apart from disagreements over specific cases there was a dispute about the autonomy and rights of social workers which professional associations were anxious to defend, as well as the rights of local authorities vis-à-vis the central authorities.

What is of interest is that both sides made appeals to the same criteria of correct authority. Each claimed that the law and the general advice of Socialstyrelsen supported their argument; that their approach was in the best traditions of solidarity and equality; and that their opponents' policies smacked of the old poor law approach. This was a dispute not between right and left. The social democrats had an absolute majority of seats over the bourgeois parties on Botkyrka Kommun, even without the support of the communist party. Girtrud Sigurdsen and even Olof Palme distanced themselves from Socialstyrelsen, itself dominated by those appointed by a social democratic government to administer social democratic policies.

Rather it seemed to be a dispute between hard and soft approaches to social policy; between the authoritarian and the libertarian. If some were intent on stamping out social security abuse, they did not say so openly. Instead the argument was about how social services could best help people to help themselves. What approach best met the needs and interests of the deprived.

Whether or not the Alby social workers were too hard on clients is difficult to tell. What is not at issue is that they thought a harder approach was justified. They thought it did clients no good to be cosseted by state benefits. Liberally-minded social workers, it was argued, did more harm than good by making weak or non-existent demands on clients. Indeed they perpetuated deprivation and inequality. Their opponents on the other hand considered that under the guise of more structure, more discipline and the distance of professionalism, Alby social workers were oppressing their clients and failed to see that a liberal approach, far from being soft, recognised the real difficulties that people faced. The liberal approach might take longer, but that process could not be artificially shortened by telling the poor to pull themselves up by their bootstraps.

In Britain the conflict over state benefits is illustrated by Norman Tebbit's suggestion to the unemployed to get on their bikes, to the outrage of socialists who claimed there were no jobs to go to. In Sweden the argument took place within the labour movement and within social work, and was about how you helped people to ride bikes and whether or not it was the responsibility of the state to provide stabilisers.

It is interesting to speculate on what made Socialstyrelsen act the way it did. It is undeniable that it failed to seek the views of social workers and it must have known that this would expose its arguments to attack. One can only conclude that its officers took a calculated risk, knowing that the Alby social workers had a coherent and well-argued case which would have the effect of diluting any criticism. While Socialstyrelsen could not prove its case by using one sided criticisms and accounts, it could draw the public's attention to what it saw as a worrying trend. The 1982 law had sought to establish a new ethos in social work services and, if Alby was indeed the tip of the iceberg, as some suspected, it was important to create a public debate about the possible consequences.

The debate itself has shown that the Alby method is hardly a localised and poorly supported phenomenon, but a viable alternative ideology to which many adhere. The law and Socialstyrelsen's advice are indeed ambiguous; probably a consequence itself of the conflicting ideologies that must have contributed to its framing. That some should continue to think that the disadvantaged might need more than voluntary help and benign persuasion; that pressure and even force might be the best way of getting them to help themselves; and that the state should aid this process, should not surprise anybody familiar with Sweden's strong temperance tradition.

The need to prevent and control alcoholism and, more recently drug-abuse, has been an important element in Swedish social policy for decades. And the issues that these problems throw up, bear a marked similarity to the issues discussed in this chapter. How do you prevent or discourage people from becoming dependent on alcohol or drugs in the first place? How do you deal with them when they do? How early should you intervene? How do you help alcoholics and drug addicts lead an independent life? Do you encourage or pressurise them to accept help and treatment?

It is interesting therefore, that the article which most strongly supported the Alby social workers, was published by *Narkotikafrågan*, the official journal of the National Association for a Drug-free Society (RNS), an organisation in favour of stronger, more coercive measures to deal with abuse. In the same issue were articles supporting Tony Manocchio and attacking leading figures in the welfare establishment (a subtle point is made by a photograph of Karl-Erik Lundgren, a key figure in Socialstyrelsen's critique of Alby, which shows him holding a drinking glass, looking a little dishevelled (*Narkotikafrågan* 1985)). In contrast, RFHL which takes a more liberal line on alcohol and drugs policy and opposes RNS, supported Socialstyrelsen (Socionomen 1985).

Bearing in mind that we have been dealing with the manifestations of a basic conflict in welfare policy, which has not been a simple dispute between the left and the right, which has reflected divisions within the labour movement itself and which has its roots in a strong temperance tradition, it is time that we looked more closely at policies to deal specifically with the problems of alcohol and drug-abuse.

CHAPTER SEVEN
Drug addiction, alcohol abuse and AIDS

INTRODUCTION

The visitor to Sweden is struck by the almost total absence of pubs or their continental equivalents. When you order alcoholic drinks with a meal, in a restaurant or a hotel, the price is prohibitive. You cannot buy strong beer, wine or spirits in a supermarket or grocery store. Instead you have to find one of the relatively few state liquor stores – Systembolaget. Systembolaget's window displays consist of advertisements for alcohol-free wine. It's motto, spola kröken means – flush spirits away, pour them down the loo.

On social occasions you become aware that Swedes are extremely reluctant to drink and drive because the penalties are so severe. Local authorities consider that to serve alcohol at civic receptions, is an unwarranted use of public money.[1] In newspapers, national and local, there is a daily concern with the problems of abuse. Articles report details of the problems, describe alternative ways of tackling them, praise the work of key figures in temperance organisations and treatment centres, and give lengthy accounts of conferences. A lot of publicity was given recently to a conference of doctors in which it was reported that three-quarters of them wanted a return to the rationing of alcohol. Quarter-page anti-alcohol advertisements, paid for by Systembolaget, depicted a healthy young male nude, whose body, it was said, could so easily be damaged by alcohol. It ends with the sentence, 'It is a crime to both procure and give away spirits, wine and strong beer to those who are under 20 years old. The punishments are fines and imprisonment'.

The visitor's first reaction is amusement or cynicism. Apart from a few obvious alcoholics on the street, with their bottles and their cans, the visible evidence of the problem is not great. The propaganda seems like a temperance hangover from the past, a puritanic spoiling of pleasure rather than a response to a genuine problem. Sweden is a well-ordered society. People on the streets look very healthy. Everywhere you see folk of all ages and both sexes cycling and jogging. Playgrounds, football pitches, ice-hockey rinks, swimming pools, ski- and athletics-tracks abound. Surely the estimate of 3–500,000 people with an alcohol problem, out of an adult population of six million is an exaggeration? As must be the fear that drugs are becoming culturally acceptable on a wide scale. Yet these matters are widely discussed and of obvious concern to many Swedes. Even the liberally aware, who feel slightly embarrassed by foreign incomprehension, are reluctant to contemplate a relaxation of the drinking restrictions, for fear that it will unleash an uncontrollable problem. That fear seems to be strongly rooted in the past.

It has already been demonstrated that temperance attitudes and traditions have influenced the development of social services, and policies dealing with children in care, contact persons and social assistance. It is now time to look more closely at those attitudes and the direct effect they have had on policies to do with alcohol and drug abuse, and, at the present time, AIDS. In this case study we will look historically at the links between the temperance and labour movements; and examine the nature of Sweden's alcohol and drug problems and some of the measure employed to tackle them. In the context of the debate about compulsion and the reform of social services legislation in 1982, we shall look at the opposing stands taken by some of the principal pressure groups and ask questions about their links with political parties. This will lead to a consideration of the controlling and restrictive way in which Örebro county proposed to deal with the drug problem, and the allegations made by young people there about the repressive means used by public officials. The chapter will end with the proposed changes to LVM that have been influenced, in part, by the emergence of the AIDS disease and the fact that the infection can be spread by drug addicts. It will be evident that while the political parties of the right seem to be solidly behind the trend to more compulsion, the left is very divided on the issue.

THE TEMPERANCE TRADITION

Heavy spirit drinking has been a cause for concern in Sweden going back generations. A religiously based temperance movement began to develop in the 1830s and 1840s, its members coming largely from the upper classes. What distinguished the modern temperance movement which developed in the years of industrialisation towards the end of the nineteenth century, was that it was a popular movement rooted in the working class. The concern was more social than religious and resulted from an alcohol problem rooted in the breakdown of community life which accompanied industrialisation (CAN 1982; p. 27 and Lundqvist 1975: p. 181).

Lundqvist described the growth of three popular movements in the first two decades of this century which had a significant impact on the political development of Sweden; the labour movement, the free church movement, and the temperance movement. Of the 230 members of the lower house of the Swedish parliament, in 1911, 51 were free church members, 87 were social democrats and 144 were absolutists. many, obviously, were members of all three. Lundqvist states that the proportion of absolutists was greatest among the social democrats compared with parties of the right. All three movements had an interest in universal suffrage and were able to cooperate politically to that end. In the 1911 parliament the social democrats demanded '... a decrease in military burdens, sweeping social reforms, energetic temperance legislation leading to statutory prohibition of intoxicating beverages' (Lundqvist 1975: p. 185). He argued that 'the temperance issue was clearly interwoven with defence and social reforms' (Lundqvist 1975: p. 185). It is for this reason that it is difficult to understand why modern Swedish socialists criticise temperance and welfare legislation prior to the 1980s as being class-based. Many social democrats would have supported the first temperance law of 1913 and the establishment of the Bratt system of rationing. Support for temperance measures was obviously something that cut across both party and class boundaries but was certainly strongly rooted within the labour movement itself.

Temperance organisations today have fewer members (400,000, which would be the equivalent of almost three million people in the UK) but they continue the study circle and youth work that began with Sweden's industrialisation. Politically too, their influence may have waned but they remain a force to be reckoned with. Indeed, at least four ministers in the present government are members of the Good Templars which means that they are totally abstinent. This combination of a powerful temperance tradition within a strong labour movement inevitably means that alcohol and drug problems have a high profile on the policy agenda. It also means that there are a

Conflict and control in welfare policy

large number of research organisations and pressure groups whose job it is to maintain a high public awareness of the scale, and costs to society, of these problems.

THE NATURE OF THE PROBLEM

The average consumption of alcohol is not high in Sweden. Compared with 37 other countries in 1983, Sweden came 31st, in the amount of alcohol consumed per capita (Centralförbundet för alkohol- och narkotikaupplysning [CAN] 1985: p. 27). In 1980 the amount for France, Spain, Italy and West Germany was over 12 litres per capita; for the United Kingdom the amount was 7.1, while for Sweden it was 5.7 (CAN 1982: p. 5). Nevertheless, it is interesting that given the much greater accessibility in this country, Sweden is not that far behind. Moreover the average level conceals a pattern of drinking and of drink-related problems that is certainly different.

Sweden came 11th in a list of spirit consumers out of 35 countries. In 1980 2.8 litres of alcohol per capita, in the form of spirits, was consumed, compared with 1.8 litres in the UK (CAN 1982: p. 5). The total number of deaths from cirrhosis of the liver, per 100,000 of the population, is also high compared with many other countries. A list of 32 countries, published by the World Health Organisation in 1979, showed Sweden lying in 18th place with a figure of 12.2 and England in 30th place with 3.9 (CAN 1985: p. 29).

One further indicator that suggests that the Swedes have a problem is in the number of people arrested for drunkenness. During the 1980s, the average number of those arrested for drunkenness, per 1000 of the population above the age of 15 was 18 – six times as great as the figure for England and Wales (CAN 1985: pp. 63-4). Although there are no doubt differences in the laws, definitions and procedures of the two countries, part of the explanation must be simply that a greater proportion of people become intoxicated in Sweden. This would seem to be confirmed by the other figures and also support the widespread stereotype that the Swedish problem consists of a small minority who drink spirits very heavily.

The evidence over time suggests that Sweden like many other countries in the postwar years has experienced a growth in average alcohol consumption. This is associated with growing affluence and the experience many Swedes have had with the drinking habits of other countries, through foreign travel. But that trend seems to have been reversed from the mid-1970s. Similarly, there has been a lot of concern about under-age young people drinking alcohol. But that growing trend has also been reversed, especially with the withdrawal of middle-strength beer from the market in 1977. Generally speaking there seems to have been a narrowing of differences in alcohol consumption between different social groups, including that of the sexes. There are few precise figures but alcohol problems among women are also becoming a cause for concern.

The temperance lobby makes a great deal of the costs of the damage done to society by drinking problems, in terms of health care, car accidents and working days lost to industry. A recent estimate that received a lot of publicity was in the order of SKR 50 billion or 8 per cent of GNP. This was compared with estimates for Finland, Switzerland and the US which ranged between 1.5 and 4.0 per cent of GNP. In a country where alcohol is expensive and difficult to find, and when you have found it, the retailer tells you to stick to alcohol-free wine, this is a remarkable achievement. While many Swedish statistics on alcohol problems are very accurate, this particular estimate is difficult to believe.

Inevitably it is difficult to find figures on the use of illegal drugs as reliable as those on alcohol but most indicators show a rise through the 1960s and 70s with a slight falling off in the 80s. Moreover it is difficult to interpret some of the increases since they might have been the result of other factors such as a decrease in leniency by police and prosecution, increases in technical and personnel resources and a growing concentration on consumers of drugs. For example, Holgersson has shown how a rise in registered drug offences between 1979 and 1982, was almost entirely due to a sudden clamp-down by the police on small dealers (Holgersson 1986: p. 7). It is interesting to contemplate that these were the very years in which there was an increase in the number of children taken into care compulsorily; the last three years of the bourgeois government.

Pressure groups have estimated that there are between 30,000 and 75,000 regular drug users (RFHL 1985: p. 8 and FMN 1985: p. 4) while heavy drug abuse, such as heroin addiction, seems to affect between 10,000 and 14,000 people (CAN 1985: p. 7). Self-report statistics based upon surveys of young people and military conscripts show that at the beginning of the 70s, approximately 15 per cent had tried illegal drugs of one kind or another. This had gone down to under 10 per cent by the end of the decade and in the mid-1980s the percentage would seem to be about 5 (CAN 1985: p. 6).

The illegality of drugs not only makes statistics unreliable but enables some pressure groups and interested parties to interpret them as they like. Some claim that the decline in self-report figures shows that the problem is diminishing, others that such figures grossly underestimate the scale of the problem. More restrictive measures that are followed by a decline in self-report figures (as happened in the example referred to by Holgersson above) could indicate either that the measures had deterred people from using drugs or that people had become too frightened to admit it.

Be that as it may, it is figures such as those referred to above that are used to justify the legislative and policy controls that are outlined in the next section.

LEGISLATION AND POLICY

Production, sales and purchase

The Swedish state has had a monopoly over retail outlets for alcohol since the end of the First World War. Until 1955 a system of rationing for those over 25 permitted a limited number of litres of spirits to be bought by men and a lesser amount by women. In restaurants men and women were permitted differentially small amounts of spirits, to be served only with meals. Ration books were abolished in 1955 since they had become ineffective but there are still many in Sweden who believe that a return to rationing is justified. Until 1977 known alcoholics were placed on a black list and random identity checks in Systembolagets were made (CAN 1982: p. 14). Through their control over licensing local authorities are able to ensure how many and what types of establishments sell alcoholic drinks. Profits from and advertising of alcoholic drinks are curtailed by the state. The state then, in its attempt to reduce alcohol consumption, has controlled the manufacture, retailing, pricing, advertising and purchase of liquor.

Scandinavians have been very strict about drinking and driving since the 1930s, long before other European countries caught on. Driving licences in Sweden can only be obtained by those with temperate habits and anybody found guilty of driving under the influence of drink to the extent that they are incapable of doing so safely, can be sentenced to prison.

The abandonment of controls of various kinds has not been very encouraging for the authorities. The year after the abolition of spirit rationing, sales went up by a third and drunkenness doubled. The attempt to encourage drinkers to switch to wine instead of spirits resulted in an increase in wine sales while spirits remained static (*Karlskoga Kuriren* 1986: p. 6). And the introduction of a medium-strength beer into ordinary retail stores caused an explosion of teenage drinking which has since diminished with the withdrawal of medium-strength beer from the market (CAN 1982: p. 6).

As to narcotics: 'The law prohibits and penalizes the possession, offering for sale, transfer, importation etc., of narcotic drugs except for medicinal or scientific use. However, the actual abuse is not punishable (Swedish Institute 1986)'. Successive changes in the law since 1968 have increased the punishment for serious drug offences to a minimum of two years and a maximum of ten years in prison. The penalty for minor offences has also increased, while in recent years there have been increasing calls from the bourgeois parties for criminalising the use or consumption of drugs (Holgersson 1986: pp. 7-8).

The temperance desire to control the supply and consumption of alcohol and drugs is obviously strong and to an extent punitive but it is equally matched by a desire to do something positive about these problems both for the sake of society and for the individuals most affected. Those addicted have to be helped.

Treatment

While the first temperance law of 1913 was concerned more with the protection of the public than with the care and treatment of alcoholics, subsequent legislation in 1931 and 1954 steadily redressed the balance. Prior to the Social Services Act of 1982, which made alcoholic problems the responsibility of the kommuns' social welfare committees, such problems had been the responsibility of local temperance boards. Describing the work of such boards, Davies and Walsh wrote:

> If a temperance board receives a complaint or otherwise finds out that someone is abusing alcohol, it will make an investigation, the outcome of which may call for remedial action. The temperance board may also decide on the compulsory commitment to a public institution for alcoholics. There are also provisions under the temperance Act to put on probation persons addicted to drink, repeatedly under the influence of drink or having undergone compulsory treatment for alcoholism.
> (Davies and Walsh 1983: p. 208)

SoL, as we have seen, put the emphasis on voluntary measures, while the Care of Alcoholics and Drug Abusers Act for adults (LVM) of the

Conflict and control in welfare policy

same year made provision for compulsory care. These replaced the old temperance legislation. SoL states that: 'The social welfare committee is to work for the prevention and counteraction of the abuse of alcohol and other habit-forming agents. Particular attention is to be paid to measures on behalf of children and young persons in this connection' (Ministry of Health and Social Affairs 1981: p. 9.). Care is compulsory where people are seriously endangering their physical or mental health through the abuse, or are liable to inflict serious harm on themselves or somebody near to them through the abuse. Social welfare committees are empowered to seek an order through the county court. Care for adults has to cease as soon as its purpose has been achieved or two months after its commencement. Young people under the age of 20, who seriously endanger their health through the consumption of drugs or alcohol, can be held for six months at a time (The National Swedish Council for Crime Prevention 1984: p. 20, and the Ministry of Health and Social Affairs 1981: p. 9).

At any one time, from 1976 to 1981, there were over 1000 adults in compulsory care and a similar number were admitted voluntarily. Compulsory admissions fell to less than 300 after the introduction of the new legislation but voluntary admissions rose to 3688 in 1983.[2] Total adult admissions for 1983 were 3917 or 6,3 persons per 10,000 of the adult population (*Statistik Årsbok* 1986: p. 311).

In keeping with the general principles of social assistance mentioned in the last chapter, there is a duty imposed on the local authorities to provide the necessary care and institutions. Under SoL the Social Welfare Committee has the responsibility to inform people of the harmful effects of abuse and to see that alcoholics and addicts get the help they need, while LVM demands that the Committee provides the institutions for those committed compulsorily. The Committee also has the responsibility of meeting a discharged alcoholic's immediate needs for housing, employment or education, and must appoint one of its officers to be responsible for contacts with the inmate. It is also the duty of public officials and physicians to bring alcoholics and drug addicts to the attention of the county administration.

In 1982 there were 24 institutions of compulsorily committed alcoholics with places for 1556 patients and 25 institutions with 815 places for those seeking admission voluntarily. In addition there were 340 places in treatment homes for drug abusers. Boarding homes for alcohol and drug-abusers are also provided by local authorities and other organisations. In 1982 there were 122 homes with 1738 places.

Moreover, health authorities provide 140 outpatient clinics for alcoholics and 20 treatment centres for drug addicts (CAN 1982: pp. 20-1).

As we saw with social assistance generally, the opportunity and obligation imposed on people to help themselves is complemented by the reciprocal obligation on the authorities to provide the necessary support, help and treatment. In the UK compulsion does not come into the care of adult alcoholics and drug-abusers, but neither are the authorities required to provide the necessary help. From an Anglo-Saxon point of view, we may shrink from the coercive measures and illiberal controls the Swedes are prepared to adopt, but on the positive side it can be said that they show more concern that we do over the damage people do to themselves through the consumption of alcohol and the taking of drugs.

The debate that has been raging in Sweden over this issue has not been about whether it is the responsibility of the state to get involved or whether the state should provide a high level of resources to the problem, but how the authorities should intervene and with what degree of force. A number of individuals, groups and organisations have taken part in this debate but four pressure groups in particular have been chosen to illustrate the dimensions of the conflict.

PRESSURE GROUPS

The four pressure groups selected have all played a significant part in the general debate about compulsion, and have done so in alliance with many other groups and individuals that cannot be mentioned here. Something first needs to be said about their origins and history and the way they relate to each other before going on to a description of their ideological and policy positions. The four are RNS (the National Association for a Drug-free Society), FMN (Parents Against Drugs), Verdandi (the Workers' Temperance Association) and RFHL (The National Association to Help Addicts).

It can generally be said that RNS and FMN would like to see a greater emphasis on compulsory and restrictive measures in welfare policy and were against the 1982 reform and that RFHL and Verdandi are very much in favour of the voluntary principle. Nevertheless, FMN cooperates with RFHL on a number of projects. FMN, RFHL and Verdandi all receive some sort of state financial support, whereas RNS jealously guards its independence. A prominent FMN member from Örebro, Peter Paul Heinemann, not only played a prominent part in the Örebro drug policy proposal, which will be dealt with later in this chapter, but has also been appointed by Girtrud Sigurdsen to the investigating committee which is recommending changes to the law concerned with addicts and alcoholics. She and the Prime Minister have both made favourable public comments about FMN, which have been interpreted by RNS as an attempt to drive a wedge between them. Certainly RNS and FMN have cooperated in producing similar policy proposals and in organising a petition in support of the criminalisation of the use of drugs, which collected 440,000 signatures in 1985 (*Narkotikafrågan* 30 1985: p. 3).

Verdandi is the oldest of the four, founded in 1896, and claims the largest membership – 50,000; RFHL began in 1964 and says it has 4,000 members; RNS, founded in 1969, claims 5,000 members; while FMN began in 1968 and says it has a membership of 10,000 people. It can clearly be seen that, with the exception of Verdandi, these organisations were all founded at about the time that drugs began to be seen as a major problem and that this coincided with the beginning of the debate about the reform of the social services. They have all been involved in that debate, then, from the start.

The accounts which follow have been collated from a variety of leaflets, policy statements and journals published by the groups themselves.

RNS

RNS considers the present welfare laws inadequate and condemns liberal attitudes towards drug use. The misguided humanitarian concern for the individual's freedom of choice and integrity can have grave consequences for young people on drugs, it argues. To allow people to experiment and to pass drugs around among themselves can only lead to greater addiction. As addiction spreads like a disease, so individuals harm themselves their families, neighbours and society as a whole. To argue, as RNS says the liberally-minded argue, that you should not intervene until addiction has become obvious, is to wait until the damage has been done. Much of the blame for lenient policies and attitudes is placed at the door of senior figures in the social services establishment, who, it claims, are out of touch with reality.

RNS claims it is better to intervene early with more forceful measures in order to prevent individuals from damaging themselves and spreading the drug habit to others. You cannot act only against the pushers and suppliers but must concentrate on the last and most important link in the chain – the consumer; for without the consumer there is no market. You cannot expect addicts to have the necessary discipline and will-power to take advantage of voluntary measures. The very nature of addiction makes it imperative that society should act responsibly to protect people from themselves. The consequences of not doing so mean that damage is done to many individuals, resources are wasted, and organised crime is encouraged to take advantage of the situation.

As far as the law is concerned it should be made clear that society cannot accept any non-medicinal use of drugs. Social services should be encouraged to intervene early where individuals are suspected of indulging in drugs. Early measures should be preventative and voluntary and include advice, support, visits from social workers and the appointment of contact persons. If this is seen to be not successful then compulsion should be used. Long-term support, supervision and treatment must be provided, whether the individual wants it or not. LVU should be changed so that an individual can be taken into care for between one and three years. The present arrangement of a six-month period of care means that a calculating individual can wait until the period is over and then return to the drug habit. Moreover the age limit should be raised from 20 to 23, as applied under the old laws.

As for LVM, RNS considers that compulsory treatment of two months is simply not enough. Experts know that it takes at least a year to help addicts overcome their problem. Again it is argued that early intervention is necessary and that there should be a scale of measures starting with the milder forms of compulsion – supervision, warnings, compulsory meeting with social workers – before finally insisting on treatment and care. Care and treatment should of course be followed by compulsory supervision and after-care to help people to acclimatise themselves to a productive, collective life. An aggressive and restrictive drug policy should be carried out at local and national levels and involve the cooperation of all authorities and voluntary organisations.

FMN

In most important respects of policy and analysis, FMN seems to be very similar to RNS. A major difference between the two associations is that whereas the latter is largely a campaigning organisation, concerned with organising meetings, marches, demonstrations and publicity, FMN is more concerned to promote support work among parents and all those who are actually related to people with a drug problem. Even those who disagree with its views respect the practical work it does with addicts. Its very motto tells us that its major concern is to help people to do something about their problems rather than wallow in them: 'The worst we can do is isolate ourselves and take on all the guilt. The best we can do is to seek fellowship with those in the same situation, and carry out a common campaign against drugs.' But its evangelical zeal at times has a tendency towards the apocalyptic. It considers that 1–2 million Swedes are on the verge of alcohol and drug abuse, which, out of a population of 8 million, is going it somewhat. It accuses Swedish tobacco manufacturers of having already designed packets and trade marks for marijuana cigarettes. It yearns for the old temperance legislation, albeit without its class bias and inadequate appeals procedures. It also claims that the abolition of the ration book for alcohol in 1955 led to a growth of pubs in Sweden analogous to the growth of mushrooms in a Swedish forest. Anyone who has actually looked for both, would say that the task of searching for mushrooms is infinitely easier.

Verdandi

Whereas RNS and FMN focus almost exclusively upon the drugs issue, Verdandi, as an old temperance association, is more concerned with the alcohol problem but sees it in the context of social structure and social policy as a whole. It sees alcoholics as victims of a competitive and unjust social order: 'We cannot accept a production apparatus which hits at all those who are unemployed, isolated and apathetic.' (Verdandi 1985).

The association exists to promote community, solidarity and fellowship through local groups, so that alcoholics have somewhere to go where they will be welcome and can engage in social activities in a drug-free environment. It actually publishes an anti-care policy but by this term it obviously means that it is against care that is imposed on alcoholics and drug addicts. While Verdandi supports increased resources for social policy, it believes that there is a danger that when experts treat the deprived as objects, they can very easily finish up being blamed for society's ills. They become scapegoats. What social policy needs to recognise is that social problems are caused by isolation, rootlessness, poverty, alienating work and unemployment. What the poor need is meaningful jobs, adequate incomes and rights to decent housing and health services. Insofar as they need help, care and treatment it should be provided on the basis of the willing cooperation of those with problems.

In Sweden, it is argued, the willingness to pay taxes and support the welfare state exists because a high standard of services is provided for all. Those who want social services that look down on clients and use controlling methods while rejecting the need for improvements in the quality of those services should realise that the consequence will be a decline in standards, a reluctance to support the tax levels that make the welfare state possible and a lowering of the status of welfare workers. This has happened in the US where there is a reluctance to pay for services reserved for the poor. This, in Verdandi's view, is exactly what those on the right would like to see. They want to blame society's ills on those with social problems, reduce sickness benefits, cut day nurseries and free abortions, attack democratic schools and the circumstances of the immigrant population and the voluntary principle in the care of alcoholics and addicts. It argues that the new moralistic demands for compulsion must not be taken seriously. Verdandi claims to be in favour of treatment that treats people as thinking, feeling, autonomous agents, not as biological machines to be programmed, governed and controlled.

RFHL

Like Verdandi, RFHL advocates the voluntary approach. And like Verdandi it suggests that the right way to study drug and alcohol problems is to look at their structural causes. Rapid industrial changes have had adverse effects on family and community life. Consumerism has supplanted traditional values. As a result many people become weak, insecure and vulnerable. The system creates such pressures that many are forced to flee from reality into the escapist world of drugs.

But, RFHL claims, it is important to get the problems into perspective. While alcohol has become socially accepted, average consumption has stabilised and is going down. Alcohol remains an age-old weapon to suppress political struggle, pacify the workers and hinder freedom. It wreaks awful damage on individuals, their families and communities but it is not a problem out of control.

A problem that deserves more attention is that of the legal drugs manufactured by the chemical industries of the western world. There is a double morality working where drugs like valium, sleeping pills, slimming tablets and stimulants of various kinds are concerned. Older people are often the victims of these drugs. There is much hidden abuse and the authorities sweep the matter under the carpet. Drugs are used to pacify prison inmates. We often complain that illegal drugs are imported from abroad, but how much damage is done in the Third World by the importation of legal western drugs? The use and abuse of legal drugs receives insufficient attention.

RFHL is suspicious of the motives of those who concentrate only on illegal drugs. It is also suspicious of those who argue for greater police powers to deal with drug-abuse. Increased use of technology, greater centralisation and professionalisation, have all led to a decrease in accountability and democratic control of the police, yet now they want to reduce people's liberties still further, using the drug problem as an excuse. What must be done is to reduce corruption within the police force itself. Large, chiefly foreign, drug companies must also be subjected to increased controls. More objective research should be carried out into their products; advertising should be limited to supplying information; and the use of generic labels rather than brand names should be encouraged.

What RFHL is arguing here is that if there is a case for more control it should be of the authorities, not the victims of intolerable social pressures. Social services itself is becoming more professionalised, remote and bureaucratised. Some social workers are beginning to make peoples' rights to social assistance conditional upon their undertaking treatment; coercive and repressive measures such as urine tests for those suspected of taking drugs are being increasingly used. The economic recession has created a climate of suspicion, means-testing and control. RFHL suggests that the right to SB might be strengthened by transferring its administration to the social insurance authorities (the SOFT proposal) leaving social workers to get on with the task of assisting people with other problems in the spirit of the SoL legislation.

As far as control in the social services is concerned, RFHL is obviously worried that the vague wording of the LVU Act leaves it open to abuse by the authorities. Every effort must be made to prevent young people from being taken into care and where this is necessary, care must be taken to ensure that good contact is kept with the individual's family. Institutions must become less like prisons and good after-care must be provided. These are sentiments which RFFR (see chapter four) would applaud.

LVM is also abused by the authorities. The courts don't follow the law and social workers do not advise people of their rights. Before the change in the legislation only alcoholics could be taken into care, now drug-abusers come under the same law. Yet RFHL does not feel that such controls should be abolished as there is wide party political and public support for them, but they should only be used where absolutely necessary and it should be recognised more strongly that it is social pressures that lead people to alcohol and drug abuse. Where the criminal law on the handling of drugs is broken, those found guilty should not automatically be sent to prison but should be given the alternative of a care contract. Supervision, treatment, education and training were better ways of dealing with drug offences than punishment.

THE POLITICS OF PRESSURE GROUPS

These differences between pressure groups at a national level show that the new legislation which came into force in 1982 did not resolve the conflict over the use of compulsion in the social services. Not only are RNS and FMN very much in favour of more forceful measures to deal, in particular, with the drug problem, but their very success and influence has led to a strong reaction from their opponents, who quite obviously feel that the gains won for the voluntary principle can so easily be lost.

At first sight, it might appear as though RNS and FMN are likely to gain most of their support from the political right while Verdandi and RFHL would have the support of the left. In a very narrow sense this is so. The bourgeois parties support the criminalisation of drug use while SAP and VPK oppose it. RNS admits that the Swedish Conservative party, of all the political parties, has the drugs policy closest to its own. Verdandi, prior to the 1985 election, claimed that there was a clear tendency in Riksdag debates, for the Conservatives to vote for the extension of compulsion; for the Centre and Liberal Parties to sometimes vote for and sometimes against; while the parties of the left tended to vote against (ALRO 1985).

As far as the pressure groups are concerned, Verdandi and RFHL seem to stress the structural inequalities in the social system and preach a more explicitly socialist message to a greater extent than do RNS and FMN. But there are reasons for this. Firstly, RNS and FMN, intend to recruit members across the political spectrum, who are united in what is basically a one-issue campaign. Secondly, members of RNS and FMN do not see drug and alcohol-abuse in structural terms. Rather they take a more behavioural approach. They argue that unemployment in the 1930s did not produce a corresponding rise in alcoholism and that the drug problem in Sweden today is concentrated in those parts of the country where there are plenty of jobs. It is not so much a question of deprivation as a question of affluence. It is commercialism which encourages addiction; it is the profits to be made that encourage drug dealers to entice people into abuse and it is the hedonism of the pop scene that tempts young people in particular to experiment with drugs. They argue that the answer to the problem, once people have become dependent upon drugs, is to ween or force them out of the habit as soon as possible. This has the virtue of being an analysis to which some socialists and some conservatives can subscribe.

Those members of RNS and FMN who are socialists – and there are many, and at the highest levels – are just as much in favour of a welfare state and full employment as are other socialists, but they do not see how you can put your faith in the expectation that long-term structural changes in society will tackle the fundamental causes of the problem, and in the meantime rely on the voluntary motivation of addicts whose freedom to act has already been impaired by their very dependence.

Although the secretary of RNS, herself a social democrat, admitted when interviewed that Conservative party policy came closest to that of RNS, she also claimed that many of its members were social democrats and people employed in the welfare system such as social workers, teachers and doctors. Nor is this denied by the opponents of RNS. On the contrary it is not only admitted that many of RNS's leading figures are socialists but it is alleged that some of them had links with the authoritarian, and now defunct, Swedish Communist Party (SKP). There are also shared ideological links with the Hassela Collective, an institution for the treatment of drug addicts, which sees its socialist task in terms of solidarity with the working class.

That some socialists are prepared to adopt policies such as those favoured by RNS, can be seen from the example of the drug programme proposal put forward by Örebro county.

THE DRUG POLICY PROGRAMME FOR ÖREBRO LÄN

In September 1984 a report was published which put forward proposals for a new policy for dealing with drug abuse in the county of Örebro (Örebro Län 1984). The group which produced the report consisted of ten people. Two were county councillors; one, a councillor representing the town of Örebro; three were officers of the town and the county; two represented the remaining boroughs in the county. The last two were representatives of FMN, one of whom was Dr Peter Paul Heinemann.

Now on both Örebro county council and the town council the social democrats and the communist party have a majority of the seats. In the county the social democrats have an absolute majority over all the other parties. It is curious therefore, that the drugs working party should include two representatives of an organisation which many on the left consider to be reactionary. It can only mean that on the issue of drug control in particular and perhaps on the issue of control in the social services in general, the social democrats are seriously divided.

Moreover the report itself reads like official RNS/FMN policy. There is the distrust of official statistics and the suggestion that the drug problem has almost reached the stage where there is a danger of drug-taking becoming culturally acceptable. This last point is based explicitly on the theories of Nils Bejerot, a leading thinker behind the policies of RNS. There is the same call for early intervention and criticism of the law on confidentiality as a hindrance to preventative work. Organisations are called on to coordinate efforts and pool information. It is even suggested that voluntary organisations which refuse to cooperate should not be given state funding.

It is suggested that different agencies should keep a watch on places where young people gather and that a register be compiled of addicts and those suspected of drug-abuse. Truancy and absenteeism from school should be watched as these are often a guise for drug-taking. While much of this has the flavour of the surveillance and victimisation attacked by Verdandi and RFHL there is also the emphasis on structural measures which they would support. The report calls for an adequate infrastructure of social security and social services for young people. There should be sufficient jobs, educational opportunities, labour market measures for the unemployed, and free-time activities to keep young people occupied. This sounds fine, but it does have rather totalitarian overtones when it is said that 'The aim must be that all young people shall take part in some form of work or study. No dropouts ought to be permitted either in school or working life . . . . No individual ought to be permitted to be outside all forms of community' (Örebro Län 1984).

It is perhaps tempered by: 'The adult world must place loving demands on the young, to show that all people need an adequate

135

society' (Ibid.). The report implies that adequate measures can only be taken if they exist in law and argues the whole time that what intervention the law does permit should be exploited to its fullest extent and legal obstacles should be got round (legally of course) where possible. The change in LVU in the summer of 1985 which made it possible to demand that young people should attend meetings with social workers or be placed under the supervision of a contact person – *intermediate force* (see Chapter 5) – should be taken advantage of. A whole chain of measures, including urine tests should be used to ensure that appropriate intervention occurs at the earliest possible time.

The social services department in Karlskoga, which is a part of the county of Örebro, criticised the document for its tone and language (Karlskoga 1986). The use of military terms like mobilisation and medical terms like epidemic, exaggerated a serious problem unnecessarily, it claimed. So did the suggestion that there was much hidden drug-abuse when all available evidence said that the problem had stabilised. Existing legislation was quite adequate and further controls were unnecessary. While extra efforts could be made to prevent young people becoming addicted to drugs there was no need to have a county-wide organisation. Existing machinery and cooperation between different agencies and organisations worked very well at a local level. To suggest that voluntary organisations might be deprived of their grants, or that organisational ways should be found round the laws on confidentiality, was wrong. The kommun response went on to attack the tendency to deny young people the right to make decisions for themselves. While in no way wishing to encourage young people to experiment with drugs, the kommun felt there was a limit beyond which the authorities should not go in interfering with the rights of young people.

Other responses varied considerably – some supporting, others criticising, some in between – reflecting the differences we have already noted at the national level. As a result of criticisms and the fact that RFHL registered a complaint with the ombudsman about certain aspects of the proposal, the final report was somewhat milder. Out came the stronger remarks about confidentiality and the funds for voluntary organisations and the overall mood is expressed in more general terms. Nevertheless, the same respect for Bejerot's theories is there and the plea for a 'chain' of measures, linked to one another by varying degrees of severity, that, despite the denials, bears an uncanny resemblance to the 'thumbscrew' steps of the old social welfare legislation. The proposal remains a document influenced more by the philosophy of RNS and FMN than that of RFHL and Verdandi (Örebro Län 1986).

Nor is the Örebro proposal merely a hypothetical blueprint. The authorities in Örebro seem to have been acting on these lines for some time. The point made earlier about the dangers of interfering too much in people's private lives was illustrated by an article in *Socialt Arbete* – a social work journal – in October 1985, entitled *The Dope Hunt (Socialt Arbete* 1985).

'THE DOPE HUNT'

The article was concerned with the experiences of young people in Örebro, who resented the way they were being treated by social workers, school counsellors, teachers and parents. It implied that they were often suspected of taking drugs simply on the basis of their lifestyle; they were blacklisted, followed and questioned by officials and expected to submit to urine tests. As a result they felt hounded in their private and social lives to such an extent that they in turn began to distrust the very authorities, including parents, who were there supposedly to help them.

Eva (14) claimed that some weeks after going to a music festival with friends who drank a little too much, she was summoned to a meeting at school attended by her parents, a social worker and the school-counsellor. The police were also there and produced photographs as evidence that Eva was mixing in bad company. Eva claimed that they suspected her of smoking hash on the basis of occasional truancy and her unconventional behaviour. She refused to submit to a urine test and as a result the suspicion deepened.

Eric, after being confronted by his father and a teacher with a list on which his name appeared as somebody suspected of being involved with drugs, was told by the school nurse that the grounds for the school's suspicion were that he played the guitar in a local rock club, often looked listless and wandered about aimlessly. Social workers followed him and his friends around town and observed them in cafés. Teachers watched for symptoms in school. He asked his father to stand up to the authorities but instead his father supported them. As a result Eric lost interest in exams and left home and school. Every time he had to go to social services for his SB, he did so with apprehension.

Others complained that they were suspected if they visited the town centre more than twice a week, and that social work field assistants would intrude on private parties. The author of the article questioned the wisdom of these actions and wondered whether they could be justi-fied in the name of a drugs campaign. He felt that they had the effect of making young people feel persecuted. They, in turn, resented and distrusted the authorities with the result that there was nobody they could turn to if they were in trouble. The campaign could actually finish up driving people into a drug environment.

The author of the article also interviewed two field assistants to get their side of the story. They claimed that they only acted on their suspicions when it was almost common knowledge that the people concerned smoked hash. One felt that little harm was done if the young people were innocent, but neither could say how many urine tests had proved positive. While denying there was any list of suspected drug-takers, they admitted that they did consider certain people at risk for whom they had a responsibility, and that early intervention was a part of local policy. In distancing himself from the practice of taking photographs of suspects in public places, one of the field workers was implicitly admitting that it went on. The author felt that while some of the things the field workers had said to him were reassuring, other statements seemed to corroborate the allega-tions of the young people. It worried him that some considered Örebro was in advance of other local authorities. Did that mean, he asked, that the rest of Sweden was on the way? The answer to that question will be given in the not too distant future.

AIDS AND CHANGES TO LVM

For many years RNS and FMN have argued that the legislation of 1982 is deficient. They suggest that between the voluntary measure of SoL and the compulsory measures of LVU and LVM, there is a gap. Moreover, the compulsory measures themselves are too weak. They have argued that the authorities must be empowered to intervene at an earlier stage and that when compulsory care is deemed to be necessary, it should be for longer periods of time and consist of more effective forms of treatment. *Narkotikafrågan*, RNS's journal, is always citing examples of the failure of the legislation and of social services departments to deal adequately with the drugs problem. It is often suggested that even those addicts who are sent to institutions,

Drug addiction, alcohol abuse and AIDS

have discovered that by being disruptive, they will be thrown out (Myrbäck 1987: p. 16). No-one, not even the police, will force them to return. This argument is obviously intended to justify even more controlling measures but it is easy to see that others might say that such behaviour is an inevitable consequence of forcing people to have treatment anyway. Without the active and voluntary co-operation of abusers, they would say, you can achieve nothing.

Nevertheless Girtrud Sigurdsen and other members of the government are clearly coming round to the view that stricter measures are necessary. The investigating commission looking at LVM, under a new chairman, and with members like FMN's Peter Paul Heinemann, has finally produced a proposal to strengthen the legislation and to lengthen the period of care for adult alcoholics and drug addicts, with the demand that all those who inject themselves with drugs, *shall* not *may* be taken into custody. While this may have happened anyway, it cannot be denied that the demand for more control has come partly from the publicity surrounding the emergence of the AIDS virus.

RNS has painted a picture of drug addicts running around spreading the AIDS virus, while organisations like RFHL have been placed on the defensive by the obvious seriousness of the problem. In an issue of *Narkotikafrågan* devoted to the AIDS problem, one article claimed that 40 per cent and more of the whole population would be affected; another insisted that the authorities had no national plan to deal with AIDS; while Bejerot insisted that mass-screening, custody and isolation were essential. He added that his own experience of treatment in a sanatorium for tuberculosis illustrated that isolation could be both pleasant and good for one's personal development! RNS, in the same issue, repeated its plea for the criminalisation of all drug-use and wondered whether there was a case for the testing of the whole population for the AIDS virus (Myrbäck 1986).

In a similar issue of its own journal, RFHL worried about the conflicts that would arise if gay men and drug addicts refused to cooperate with measures that were forced upon them. How much tolerance existed amongst the population that felt threatened, it wondered. Would it be possible to influence general public understanding with information about risk groups (*Slå Tillbaka* 5 1985). Nevertheless, after some heart-searching and debate amongst the membership, RFHL finally came down firmly in its continued support for voluntary measures and the free supply of syringes. The importance of tackling AIDS realistically was seen to override the possibility of the fact that free needles might be seen as condoning drug abuse (Lindgren 1987).

Another article said that AIDS was already a notifiable disease in Sweden and that anybody suspected of carrying the virus could be forced to have a test. Although a spokesman for the Ministry of Social Affairs claimed that it would be people's behaviour, rather than their membership of risk groups such as gay men, prostitutes and drug addicts, that would be the criterion for intervention, it was felt that in practice this distinction might not amount to much (Nilsson, I. 1985: p. 10). Another article, looking at Denmark's more severe AIDS problem, said that the Danes would not countenance the compulsory care and punishment of those infected with the AIDS virus, measures which were regarded in Denmark as 'typically Swedish' (Nilsson M, 1985, p. 36).

AIDS then has sharpened the debate about the extension of compulsory measures against alcohol and drug abuse. With the new report by the investigating commission into LVM, the scene was set for a controversial debate at the SAP conference in 1987.

THE 1987 SAP CONFERENCE

Political parties in Sweden hold their conferences, not annually, but every three years in preparation for the next general election. The 1987 conference decided the position of the SAP on a whole range of issues one year prior to the general election of 1988. The motions that were to be debated showed that the battle lines had already been drawn. There were motions to strengthen the rights of individuals under LVU and LVM; there were motions for and against a greater emphasis on control and compulsion; there were motions to attack the spread of AIDS by a variety of means. There were also attempts by the governing body of the party to lessen or mediate the resulting conflict (Partistyrelsens Förslag 1987).

As far as the compulsory care of alcohol and drug abusers was concerned, the Conference passed the motion to lengthen the maximum period of care from two months to six. Legislation to this effect is expected to be placed before the Riksdag and to be passed in the Summer of 1988.

CONCLUSION

The evidence on alcohol consumption in Sweden is ambiguous.

While average consumption is low compared with many countries, other indicators suggest there may be a serious problem. However it may simply be that a strong temperance tradition has helped to create a powerful lobby within the medical profession, the welfare bureaucracy and pressure groups which exaggerates the scale of the problem. It is even more difficult to pronounce on the consumption of drugs, since illegality makes the collection of reliable statistics impossible. Nevertheless it is clear that there is widespread concern about the abuse of alcohol and drugs in Sweden. However there are fundamental differences between the 'voluntary' and 'compulsory' camps about the causes of the problem and how to deal with them. Moreover the two camps do not correspond with the political left and the political right. While those on the right are more likely to want to see LVM and LVU strengthened, the period of compulsory care for abusers lengthened, and the criminalisation of drug use, this is more uniformly true for conservatives than it is for members of the Centre and Liberal parties. Those on the left are also divided on the issue. Some socialists take the line that more control and compulsion will be ineffective and indeed, counter-productive; others feel that the problem is too immediate and destructive to rely on the voluntary motivation of individuals to seek help and treatment.

It is also clear from all four case studies, that the preoccupation with drug and alcohol abuse in Sweden has implications for other aspects of welfare policy. It was suggested in Chapter 4 that the numbers of children in care and the numbers confined to institutions for the mentally-ill might be disproportionately affected by the concern for drug and alcohol-abuse. A similar tendency was noted in Chapter 5 concerning the use of contact persons. In Chapter 6 it was pointed out that there were many links between the Alby approach to dependence on social assistance and the concern with drug and alcohol-dependency. And in Chapter 7 we have seen how the AIDS issue is also being linked with the debate about the care and treatment of drug addicts.

But this preoccupation by some individuals and groups is challenged and opposed by others. Control in welfare policy certainly exists, but it has been the subject of considerable debate and conflict. It is to the analysis of control and conflict generally that we must now turn in Part three.

NOTES

1. I attended a full council meeting in Karlskoga Kommun during my stay there, and was surprised by the brevity and formality of debate. When I asked afterwards whether they ever had lengthy, informal debates I was told that the last such occasion was when they had discussed the issue of whether public money should be spent on alcohol for official receptions.
2. This rather suggests that the replacement of the old temperance law by LVM had the effect of reducing compulsory care while at the same time encouraging more people to take advantage of voluntary treatment.

PART THREE
Conclusions

CHAPTER EIGHT

Critiques of Swedish welfare

INTRODUCTION

It has already been demonstrated that Sweden can legitimately be regarded as possessing a welfare state which is, in many respects superior to others. Yet the evidence of the history of Sweden's social services up until 1982, shows that a high degree of social control in welfare policy existed. The case studies suggest that marked vestiges of that control have persisted into the 1980s in spite of the liberalising campaign mounted by reformers throughout the 1970s and the changes in legislation that took place in 1982.

A number of writers have attempted to explain the degree of control that exists in social welfare in particular and in Swedish society in general. Four have been selected for closer examination in this chapter. It will be seen that they represent a wide range of political perspectives and account for the relationship between welfare and control in markedly different ways. Leif Holgersson's work is that of a supporter of the social democratic welfare state who explains the controlling aspects of welfare policy in terms of a hangover from the past; Kurt Sjöström's neo-marxist analysis sees the controlling features of Swedish society in terms of capitalism's need to control the labour force; Ronnby's anarchistic study takes an even more critical view of the way in which the technocrats of the labour movement have joined forces with capitalism to create a state apparatus that controls every aspect of people's lives; while Arthur Shenfield's conservative critique is an attack upon the controlling features of Swedish socialism and the detrimental effect socialist policies have had upon the free enterprise economy.

Conflict and control in welfare policy

HOLGERSSON: A SOCIAL DEMOCRATIC CRITIQUE

In *Socialvård* Holgersson describes the history and development of
social welfare policy in Sweden, its poor law origins and how little it
changed in the early decades of social democratic rule. He discusses
the dissatisfaction that led to the setting up of the investigating
commission in 1968 and its shadow, the cooperative committee, SSM
(see Chapter 3), that campaigned so hard for a liberalising of welfare
legislation. From the beginning of the book it is clear that
Holgersson's views have much in common with SSM. He is very
critical of the use of compulsion in Swedish social services. He
describes the work of the Commission, its various reports and the
conflicts that arose during its time of office and concludes with a
critical assessment of the new legislation of 1982.

It is important to see Holgersson's work not as an impartial,
historical account but as a rallying cry to the doubters within the
labour movement who after the years of discussion and conflict still
worried about the wisdom of abandoning the use of compulsion. The
first edition came out at a crucial time during the Commission's
deliberations, just when the bourgeois government was beginning to
drag its feet. It was intended to show socialists just which side they
should be on. The last edition appears to have come out after SoL and
LVU had been passed but before LVM which although it reduced the
duration and limited the criteria for care nonetheless retained
compulsory powers over alcoholics and extended them to drug
addicts.

It may be that in order to convince fellow social democrats in
particular that compulsion should be abandoned Holgersson had to
convince them that compulsory care was very 'unsocialist'. Reformers
like Holgersson were convinced that the old welfare laws were class
laws, an inheritance from Sweden's poor law past. The temperance
law in particular, was seen as repressive and punitive. Moreover it was
unnecessary and inefficient. Unnecessary, he explains, because other
laws existed on the statute books which could be used to protect
individuals and society from any immediate damage that might be
done to them by an alcoholic. Inefficient since people with severe
alcohol problems were not going to be cured of their addiction by
force; on the contrary it was likely to make matters worse.

The important thing was first to recognise that addiction had
social causes and second to persuade the individual to voluntarily
seek help and treatment. This, Holgersson argued, was contrary to
the repressive, charity, work ethic traditions of social welfare in the

past but in keeping with the group solidaristic tradition of the labour movement that had produced the welfare state. He cites the early sickness funds which workers collectively organised in the early stages of industrialisation as an example.

This type of social policy grew among the poor themselves out of needs which were experienced as common to all. Sickness funds and other similar arrangements came to be experienced early on as a real security by the funds' members, even if the amount of compensation was small. These forms of democratic help were to give ideas to the trade union movement and to the SAP which in the twentieth century were to have such an influence on Swedish social policy. (Holgersson 1981: p. 76)

In Holgersson's view the establishment of the welfare state in the 1930s and 40s, in terms of sickness insurance and pensions, housing and labour market policy, embodied the group solidaristic tradition of the labour movement in a way that the welfare services for the poor did not. It is this part of his study which, although persuasive, is not entirely convincing.

He claims that in the early development of Sweden's social policies the labour movement was intent on establishing full employment, social insurance for all and health services for all. It was intended that these should reduce the numbers of people who would need to apply for social assistance. If people had a right to a job, a right to a decent pension, free hospital care, family allowances, then this was not only the best way of tackling poverty but made the reform of the poor law, the child care law and the temperance legislation less pressing. He also argues that the sheer effort demanded to achieve major welfare reforms and bring about the structural and economic changes in the decades following 1932 distracted the attention of the trade unions and the SAP from the needs of those who fell through the safety net of the welfare state. It was felt, or rather hoped, that the problem would slowly disappear (Holgersson 1981: pp. 134, 157, 190).

Now as an explanation as to why the social democrats did not give immediate attention to class-based and repressive welfare legislation and the issue of compulsion in the 1930s and 40s, Holgersson's account is convincing. But how the temperance law of 1955, the social help law of 1956 and the child care law of 1960 could have remained relatively uninfluenced by the group solidaristic traditions of a labour movement that had consolidated its political and economic power over two decades is a bit more difficult to swallow. And as an explanation of why the authorities in Sweden can still be accused of the excessive use of compulsory care, how social democratic Botkyrka could accept the Alby interpretation of SoL,

147

Conflict and control in welfare policy

how social democratic Örebro could take such a harsh line on drug
addicts, how social democratic Riksdag representatives could be
induced to vote for LVM and mellan tvång, and how the 1987 SAP
conference was able to approve of an extension of the period of
compulsory care for alcoholics and drug addicts, the theory is most
unhelpful.

The flaw in Holgersson's account may however have been
deliberate. As an ardent campaigner against compulsory measures in
social services and as the editor of a committed social work journal, he
must have known that many of his opponents in the debate were
fellow socialists. Yet something led him to argue that compulsory
measures had no place in the traditions of the labour movement and
that even the reforms of the 1950s were class-based and rooted in
Sweden's repressive poor law. On the one hand, his book may have
been no more than an ideological ploy; an attempt to convince others
that the reformers were the true representatives of working class
interests. On the other hand, it may be that Holgersson genuinely
believes that those socialists who favour compulsion are not really
socialists at all – that their authoritarian tendencies actually nullify
any pretensions they may have to being socialists and that they are
really reactionaries in disguise.

SJÖSTRÖM: A NEO-MARXIST CRITIQUE

Sjöström solves Holgersson's dilemma by taking a much more
critical view of the welfare state as a whole. He sees it as an institution
which may have resulted from the political pressures of the labour
movement, but one which because it functions within the constraints
of a capitalist economy, has come to meet the needs of the capitalist
system and the interests of the bourgeoisie. The controlling elements
are repressive and reactionary, according to Sjöström, for the same
reason.

In spite of decades of social democratic governments, he claimed in
a paper written at the end of the 1970s, Sweden remained an unequal
society in which 5 per cent of the population owned 50 per cent of the
wealth (Larsson and Sjöström 1979: p. 172). The economic power of
families like the Wallenburgs and individuals like Per Gyllenhammer,
the managing director of Volvo, was considerable. Moreover what
greater equality of opportunity existed could be dismissed as merely
meritocratic. It still resulted in the basic division of labour and the

hierarchical reward structure that capitalism required. What re-distribution did take place was horizontal rather than vertical; it took place between groups in the same class (young to old; employed to unemployed; healthy to sick). Social policy was seen then as having a '...dampening effect on the most critical issues. Social policy contributes to making objective class boundaries diffuse and unclear. Those "solutions" achieved by social services are most often pseudo-solutions which neither alter the causes of the needs nor their economic basis' (Larsson and Sjöström 1979: p. 174).

Sjöström in a later work, *Socialpolitiken*, argues that the reforms which followed the capitalist crisis of the 1930s can no longer provide the principles on which to act in response to the crisis of the 1980s. The solidaristic wage policy has benefited large capitalist firms at the expense of small ones. The same can be said for the initially radical proposal on the state's earnings-related pension schemes (ATP). Not only has capitalism used the pension funds directly or indirectly but what pensioners have gained in their pockets on the one hand has been taken away by the local authorities in increased charges on the other. He seems to imply that as long as the state is not in the hands of the workers, even the most radical of reforms becomes absorbed by and ultimately exploited by capitalist interests (Sjöström 1984). Moreover the internationalisation of capitalism and in particular Swedish capitalism means that there is a big question mark in the future over the possibilities of future Swedish governments being able to control the economy to the extent that they have in the past. Major Swedish companies have more employees abroad than they have at home and have factories scattered all over the world (Sjöström 1984: p. 124).

Sjöström recognises many of the real gains in working-class living standards that social democratic reforms have achieved, but insists that this has not been without considerable cost and that the future prospects for the working class look very fragile indeed. Cooperation with capitalism has meant that the process of modernisation and rationalisation has been aided by the trade unions who have delivered a disciplined work-force into the hands of employers. The economy is still basically in private hands. The welfare state, it is argued, must be seen as a contradictory institution which while it undeniably gives security to the work-force has also aided private capital to manipulate the work-force. There are restrictions on striking and for many years unemployed workers were almost forced to move to areas of higher employment. Social services penalise and punish the working class disproportionately and help adapt the casualties of capitalism to the

Conflict and control in welfare policy

very system that has damaged them. In other words the social democratic welfare state has been a controlling agent for the employing class.

Writing in the 1970s, Sjöström complained about the 'increase in the janitorial demands on social services' (Larsson and Sjöström 1979: p. 178). He insisted that the child care and temperance laws were disproportionately applied to the working class. Working-class children were punished for infringements of the law for which children from middle-class families would be let off. He quoted a piece of research from the 60s to illustrate how the same tendency existed in the treatment of alcoholics.

Table 8.1 Persons (men) who were subject to the temperance authority's measures. Socio-economic group in percentage compared to gainfully employed men in the country

	Subject to temperance authority's measures	Gainfully employed men in the country (1960)
Entrepreneurs	7	20
Salaried employees	7	26
Workers	75	53
Others (including temporary workers and those without a job)	11	1

Source: Larsson and Sjöström 1979: p. 176.

Social services, he argued, patched up social problems and neither tackled their causes nor provided solutions. They sought to modify people's behaviour and attitudes by rewarding the conformist and punishing the deviant. Another criticism made by him was that social assistance was minimal and in no way compensated a family for the lack of decent child care facilities which would enable the mother to be independent and earn a living. Sjöström went on to describe the setting up of the investigating commission in 1968 and complained that although its aims seemed comprehensive it was distrusted by social workers and their organisations (Larsson and Sjöström 1979: p. 179). In a later work Sjöström seems to have changed his mind and praises the work of the Commission: 'The result of the social investigation, the social services law (SoL), was above all an adaptation of the practice that had already been developed at a local level. One of the fruits of the work and ideas of the Commission was

Critiques of Swedish welfare

however that the state's repression of the socially rejected was lessened through the reduction in compulsory measures,' (Sjöström 1984: p. 142).

What is interesting about these comments is that the social services can be characterised as being repressive in an almost monolithic way in one work, while in another it is admitted that major improvements have been made in response to innovations at a local level. Sjöström's dilemma, like that of other neo-marxists, is that while lip-service is paid to the relative autonomy of the state and the success of labour movements in advancing the interests of the working class, it is often little more than that because the premise on which his argument is based is that a capitalist system primarily serves capitalist interests. The values and interests that underpin the welfare state, are capitalist values and interests. The controlling aspects of the system are therefore capitalist. But if *welfare services* can be contradictory and capable of serving the interests of the ruling class and working class alike, why cannot the same be said for the *controlling* aspects of the system? Might it not be that the Swedish labour movement, those employed to run and administer welfare services and indeed the working class itself have also fought for social control within the welfare state? The left is given credit for the liberating aspects of the system, but it is the right that is blamed for the controlling elements.

Surely this must be partly due to the fact that Sjöström's ideology leads him to believe that the ideal to which he is dedicated is that of a classless society, one supposedly free from conflict and therefore the need for control. Yet if he were to examine the experiences of existing socialist societies he would find not only a need for control but very strong measures not dissimilar to those proposed by socialist advocates of greater stringency in welfare policy in his own country. As a socialist he does not seem to be willing to concede that some socialistic elements within the state welfare apparatus may be inherently controlling. To this extent his argument is not dissimilar to that of Holgersson, but it is one that stands in stark contrast to that of Ronnby.

RONNBY: AN ANARCHIST CRITIQUE

While many neo-marxists can see the positive side of some welfare measures within capitalism and can imagine themselves using similar means and similar policies in a socialist state, a much more

151

critical line is taken by Ronnby. Although Ronnby's *Socialstaten* takes Marx's concept of alienation as its starting point, his attack on the Swedish welfare state is more anarchistic in flavour and in its prescriptions.

He basically sees the whole state apparatus as a dominating and controlling one. The trade unions and the voluntary organisations have been drawn into an authoritarian institution which serves both the interests of modern capitalism and of the professional and managerial class. The new ruling class is different from the traditional bourgeoisie, he says, and includes all those who are united in a management community to protect their economic and political power. Whereas the early capitalist state had sovereign control over society, in late capitalism the social state has what he calls a 'superior influence' (Ronnby 1985: p. 106). So while he suggests that the ruling class of today is more broadly based and less homogeneous than in the past, its influence and pervasiveness are greater.

He goes on to argue that the mass of the population has been stripped of any vestige of influence or power outside the three-year visit to the ballot-box, where the choice is between four main parties who, partly financed by the state compete to control the state machine. Trade unions control their members, not the other way around; the same goes for the national organisations 'representing' tenants and pensioners. Local authorities and consequently local councillors have been so reduced in number that very few people can actively participate in the political life of their areas. The whole trend of authoritarianism is to discourage participation of ordinary people while maintaining the façade of representative democracy.

Ronnby's view of the welfare system is equally uncompromising. À la Illich he claims that education, employment, housing, health care and social work institutions have taken away people's right and ability to care for themselves and each other. Whole areas of everyday human life have been monopolised by the social state's professionals and managers. People are lonely and isolated and without the support of extended families and community. As a result they become dependent upon the impersonal services and support of bureaucratic experts. The rationalisation, centralisation and urbanisation of society at large are mirrored in the processes that have transformed social policy. People are discarded by the system and patched up by the system. They have no independent existence outside the system.

He argues that there are three lines of action in Swedish social policy – income support, adaptation and care. Because the state now takes care of income support, employers do not have to worry about the effects of discarding people. They won't starve. By adaptation policy he implies that in education and in behaviouristic forms of treatment, the state ensures that people adapt to the system. It is the system's needs which are paramount, not the individual's. Care policy simply ensures that capitalism has a more flexible work-force. Because the state is prepared to look after young children, the elderly and the handicapped, those relatives, friends or neighbours who would have done so are free to become employees (Ronnby 1985: Chapter 3). As more married women become employed the expectations of all married couples rise with the result that a one-income family has a very low standard of living compared with a two-income family. Not only does the state move in to meet the demand for increased child care places but also with various income-maintenance schemes to protect the family income in the event of illness and provide for parental leave of absence and unemployment. Ronnby describes a situation in which the family becomes increasingly dependent on a social wage provided by the state.

Ronnby returns again and again to the theme of the two-income family. He points to the anomaly of women being employed to do the very jobs for someone else, that they used to do for their own families; the difficulties and pressures of family life when you have two parents at work; the advantages of informal care based on love as opposed to formal care based upon a cash relationship. At no point does he mention the possibility that many women may prefer the present arrangement with the freedom and independence it gives them. All the time he emphasises that the development of state social services is a way of releasing women for the labour market while catering impersonally for those the labour market has no need for – the old, the young, the handicapped.

Even the reorganisation of social services is seen as insidious. It is not a progressive reform of an old system but a centralisation and a rationalisation by technocrats who want to ensure that social services are planned with feed-back and evaluation systems. The treatment technology that clients are subjected to is based upon the assumption that 'One can direct and govern behaviour and attitudes so that social processes can be pre-planned. In such a system clients tend to be transformed into treatment objects. Clients become social products which different care teams investigate while they are slushed round in a care chain' (Ronnby 1985: p. 81).

He regards the reform of social services as an attempt to make everyone dependent upon the social state and no-one else. He quotes Sven Aspling, the Minister for Social Affairs in the early 1970s and a critic of the compulsory approach, as saying that people will no longer have to be directed to relatives or seek the benevolence of private individuals since the local kommun will provide help, advice, support, care as well as money, therapy and treatment. This was clearly intended by the Minister to reassure people about their rights to state help. Ronnby interprets it as meaning that the state was seeking to supplant all forms of private help and support. Whereas Sjöström saw the absence of good child care facilities as something which excluded poor families from the chance to earn a decent income (Larsson and Sjöström 1979: p. 175), Ronnby argues that child care is a device to force women out to work.

Ronnby would like to see a much more communal society in which people worked for fewer hours and had more time to devote to caring for and sharing with each other. They would help each other with their problems. They would care for their children, the elderly and the handicapped. They would self-manage the estates in which they lived, they would have greater control over the economic enterprises for which they worked. They would have a guaranteed minimum income which would enable them to choose between employment and work for the community. What I think Ronnby's analysis suffers from is a nostalgic romanticism. Small is beautiful in Ronnby's eyes. Families, communities and workshops are 'good', as are friends, relations and neighbours; cities, bureaucracies and experts are 'bad'. His ideal world would seem to have no place for the major health, education, housing and social insurance programmes that are an inevitable feature of the welfare state.

A number of interesting points arise from Ronnby's work. The very use of the term social state (a term borrowed from German marxists and therefore not necessarily applicable to Sweden) implies a monolithic and uncaring institution. Ronnby quite deliberately avoids the use of the concept of a welfare state. He encapsulates all teachers, social workers and doctors within the term technocracy, thus again implying something monolithic. Even the trade unions and the labour movement hierarchy become part of a conspiracy to control the work-force.

Ronnby seems to regard social control as such a pervasive feature of the social state that he makes little reference to the debate about compulsion as such. But he does liken the socialist theories of Bejerot, the philosophy of the Hassela Collective (an institution for drug addicts which Bejerot and other socialists helped to found) and the activities of RNS to the brainwashing behaviourism of the Soviets. He goes further and suggests that although they and many social workers adopt what they describe as a socialist, and comradely approach to addicts and alcoholics, in practice they use force to compel someone to do something against his or her will through the use of the state's formal control apparatus. So, not only are those behind the reform of the social services part of the social state, but those opposed to the reforms are also part of the social state. Ronnby, more than any other critic of Swedish social policy, reduces the welfare state to a controlling machine. The controllers consist not only of all employers, shareholders, managers and professionals; not only of all teachers, social workers and doctors; but even those who 'run' the labour movement itself.

Ronnby's critique then, enables us to see that the elements of control in Swedish welfare policy may not only be the consequence of capitalist manipulation but also of the managerial class interests of social democratic politicians, leading trade union figures and state technocrats. The latter become not simply the dupes of the system, as Sjöström would have us believe but active, cooperative participants. Unfortunately however, by emphasising the interests of a wider and more powerful ruling class, Ronnby has to totally neglect the positive side of major welfare programmes and policies. In exactly the same way that Ivan Illich attacked schools as manipulative institutions regardless of whether they embodied progressive or traditional approaches to education (Illich 1971), so Ronnby would have us see Swedish social services as manipulative and controlling regardless of whether the emphasis was upon a voluntary or a compulsory approach. The possibility of welfare services and welfare personnel being humane, caring and benevolent seems to be ruled out by definition. But it would require a tremendous act of faith to believe that his romantic, community-based alternative could in the near future be a substitute for the major welfare programmes of a modern industrial state, be it capitalist or socialist.

It is interesting to note that Ronnby's extreme libertarian views lead him to see welfare state socialism as just as controlling in many respects as the right-wing perspective of Arthur Shenfield would have us believe.

SHENFIELD: A CONSERVATIVE CRITIQUE

Those who believe in the virtues of the free market and the need for unfettered private enterprise naturally enough complain that the

Conflict and control in welfare policy

Swedish system is stifling the will to work and invest. Marginal and average tax rates are said to be too high and state regulation of businesses excessive. In consequence there has been a decline in the number of small firms and the black economy is rampant. High sickness and unemployment benefits, it is said, make it unnecessary for many to work. Dependence on state services and benefits stifles the motivation and willingness of people to provide for themselves and their families. If the state provides health care, housing and education then individuals are prevented from exercising their free choice. It is said that swollen state bureaucracies are over-staffed and inefficiently run. The Swedish welfare state is seen as an experiment in socialism which seeks to brainwash the population into accepting a system that deprives them of their individuality.

Shenfield, who has argued in this fashion, complains, for example, about the kind of training that 'workers' representatives' (his emphasis) receive at the hands of the Workers' Educational Association (ABF):

> ... which is a blatantly anti-capitalist and pro-socialist body. The 'representatives' must be given paid leave of absence from work to attend the ABF programmes, which means that their companies are required to finance propaganda against themselves. Incidentally compulsory Swedish language training for immigrant workers is also handled by the ABF. It is not difficult to imagine the effect of the ABF's indoctrination on industrial relations with these workers and on their introduction to Swedish society. (Shenfield 1980)

He also alleges that the welfare state, far from solving social problems, increases them. He points to Sweden's one-parent families, the increase in divorce, its growing crime rate and the abuse of drugs as evidence of social and moral malaise. Vandalism of public buildings, suicide and alcoholism among young people are growing, he claims. Shenfield asserts that, had the golden goose of the Swedish economy been allowed to lay golden eggs, unhampered by left-wing politicians, trade unionists and bureaucrats, then the Swedish people would have had a level of welfare superior to that supplied by the state.

The control that Shenfield objects to principally is the control that the Swedish state exercises over the resources of private companies and private individuals. Linked with the control of resources is that exercised by the state on people's right to choose the type of education, health care and social insurance they want. Another kind of control that Shenfield complains about is the control that a socialist state has over a citizen's civil liberties. Indeed he would argue that control in the latter sphere is an inevitable consequence of control in the other areas. It is in totalitarian terms that Shenfield sees the present Swedish state. Through high taxation and the state's monopolistic provision of services individuals become dependent upon the state for too much. Their children have to go to day nurseries, they have to be taught socialist values, they have to have medical and psychological check-ups, their inadequacies have to be treated, they are compelled to have care.

From the stand-point of a perfectly functioning free-market economy, in which Shenfield clearly believes, he has a case. State intervention and trade union power do distort market mechanisms. The welfare state and full employment can only be maintained by increasing degrees of control over resources and individual and corporate property rights. But where is this perfectly functioning system? What value is there in comparing a real society with an ideal type? Surely a more realistic comparison should be with a society in which free enterprise has been given a much freer reign, like the US. Would Shenfield seriously ask us to believe that social problems in Sweden compare unfavourably with those of the US? Poverty, bad housing, urban decay, drug addiction and unemployment are all much more widespread in America. Moreover recent evidence would suggest that the Swedish economy is just as efficient as that of the US (*Economist* 1987), and that the Swedish welfare state ensures that the mass of the population suffers less material deprivation and has more security than its American counterpart. If greater controls exist over the lives of individual Swedish citizens then this has to be set against the ability of the system to maintain full employment and provide a generous standard of living for the vast majority of the population – something the US clearly fails to achieve.

Insofar as Shenfield makes us question the more glossy and idealistic picture we often get of Sweden, his analysis is useful. State intervention can be counter-productive and a large public sector may have an adverse effect on the wealth-producing capacity of the economy. Trade unions and welfare bureaucrats may pursue sectional interests which are not in the public interest. Welfare agencies and policies may create more problems than they solve and must therefore be considered as an intrinsic part of social problems and not simply as their solution. There may indeed be authoritarian elements in Swedish social democracy not dissimilar to those found in Soviet communism.

The plausibility of Shenfield's case when it was written at the end of the 1970s lay in the fact that the Swedish economy was in some difficulty. But even then, there was no justification for comparing Sweden with a perfect, free-market economy. Free markets have always had imperfections and some degree of state intervention has always been necessary to correct those imperfections. The real argument should be about whether the degree of state intervention in Sweden has made the economy more or less effective and whether it has resulted in more or less social and economic problems than in other capitalist societies. Swedish society has imperfections, but these should be compared with the imperfections faced by other capitalist societies and their achievements should also be compared.

Moreover Shenfield's attack on state intervention should not be allowed to conceal the fact that governments of the right are only too happy to employ controlling measures when it suits their purposes. When the policies that people like Shenfield advocate, result in increasing unemployment and poverty, as they often do, there are many on the right who would ruthlessly use the power of the state to control those who become dependent on social assistance. Peregrine Worsthorne, an English political commentator, expressed his distaste for the liberal thinking of free-marketeers like Shenfield when he wrote:

> People are going to have to be re-taught to stand on their own two feet, and weened off the habits of dependence. And a culture restored which strengthens family life. The free play of the market is not going to do any of these things. Only the state, exploiting every part of its potential power – fiscal, educational, administrative and even coercive – will be strong enough to work this transformation.   (Worsthorne 1983)

And from another article:

> The urgent need today is for the state to regain control over the people, to reassert its authority, and it is useless to imagine that this will be helped by some libertarian mish-mash drawn from the writings of Adam Smith and John Stuart Mill, and the warmed-up milk of 19th century liberalism.   (Worsthorne 1978)

These sentiments are unashamedly authoritarian and there is no way whereby they can be dismissed as socialistic. Arthur Sheldon would have us believe that socialism is inherently controlling and capitalism inherently liberating. The truth of the matter is that Sheldon and Worsthorne present us with two very contrasting views of what conservatism is about. Behind the conservative's ideological façade of freedom and choice, there are class interests which are prepared to use the power of the state to control the deviant, the rebellious and the deprived, a fact that is reinforced by the role that conservatives in Sweden, as we have already seen, have played throughout the debate about compulsory measures in the social services.

CONCLUSION

Each of the critiques discussed above draws our attention to phenomena that can help us make sense of the degree of social control within Swedish welfare policy; historical developments and continuities, the need for capital to control labour, the power of welfare bureaucrats and professionals, and the totalitarian potential of state socialism. But the political partiality of the authors and the internal logic of their theories seem to lead them to ignore or understate important material which would weaken their arguments. Holgersson, who has been very involved in the debate about compulsion for many years, is intent upon arguing that control and compulsion have no place in the traditions of the labour movement, yet we have seen that some of the advocates of more controlling measures are not only socialists themselves but they insist that it is they who represent the true traditions of the labour movement and not the liberalising reformers. Sjöström, because he wishes to advance the case for a socialist society, has to attribute the controlling aspects of the welfare state to the imperatives of a capitalist system. It therefore follows that those socialists who are caught up in the state apparatus find themselves having to implement policies with which, as socialists, they have no sympathy. Ronnby's belief in maximum individual autonomy leads him to be critical of all bureaucratic, hierarchical structures whether they be capitalist or socialist – any state, by definition, is repressive and controlling. While Shenfield, in order to defend free enterprise and individual property rights, is forced to be suspicious of any form of socialist collectivism.

Whereas the partiality of Holgersson can easily be understood in the context of his immediate involvement in the political debate concerning the reform of Swedish social services legislation, that of the other writers is a consequence of the utopian assumptions upon which their theories are built. Implicitly, each of them has a belief in a perfect social order alongside which the Swedish welfare state pales in comparison. Shenfield's model society is that of a free enterprise economy based upon perfect competition, the functioning of which requires as little state involvement in the economy as possible; Sjöström assumes the future possibility of a classless society in which

159

Conflict and control in welfare policy

the means of production are owned collectively, not privately; while Ronnby envisages a harmonious social order freed from the domination of private and public bureaucracies. Although it is perfectly legitimate to compare the deficiencies of real systems with the merits of ideal ones, it is not a procedure that helps make much sense of the data that has been the core of this book.

In order to apply some of the insights gained from these critiques to an analysis of control in welfare policy, while avoiding the problems arising from their partiality, two things need to be done. Firstly, we need to develop a framework that will enable us to recognise that the controlling aspects of welfare policies cannot be attributed solely to the forces of the left, socialists and the welfare state on the one hand or to the right, conservatives and capitalism on the other. This will be attempted in the next chapter.

Secondly, we need to relate the conflict about control, that the case studies revealed, to the context of a welfare state which compares very favourably with state welfare in other capitalist countries even if it falls short of the utopian expectations of some critics. This will be attempted in the last chapter of the book.

CHAPTER NINE
Analysis

INTRODUCTION

The aim of this chapter is to present a framework which will help us account for the nature and dynamics of the conflict concerning control in Swedish welfare policy and to argue that such a framework could be developed to provide an explanatory theory for similar conflicts within capitalist society generally. It will begin with the case for amending conventional political analyses, in which issues of inequality are superimposed upon issues of control, so that inequality and control issues can be analysed separately.

THE AUTHORITARIAN/LIBERTARIAN SPECTRUM

As was seen in the previous chapter, there is a tendency within political debate to place a great deal of emphasis upon left/right distinctions. Political differences are often explained in terms of this spectrum. The inevitable consequence is that the opposition is always seen as being to the right or the left of whichever position we occupy. Socialists must be the principal enemies of capitalism and capitalists the major obstacles to socialism, while those in the centre complain of the extremism of both sides. But what is meant by this distinction? It is largely a question of orientation towards the ownership of property and wealth and its implication for the degree of material inequality that exists in society. Those on the right wish to preserve private rights to property ownership, those on the left stress the importance of public or communal ownership (not

161

necessarily state ownership), and those in the centre wish to preserve some sort of balance between the two.

At any one point on the spectrum we find a number of groups and factions in competition with each other; each vying for power and influence; each claiming to be better or truer representatives of a desirable social system and the interests of the mass of the population. Inevitably the temptation exists for each faction to not only blame 'the enemy' but also to associate rival factions with 'the enemy'. Advocates of free market economics refer to all state collectivism, even that favoured by governments of the right, as creeping socialism; hard-line right wingers describe any kind of liberalism as pinko; to an anarchist or a Trotskyist, Soviet socialism is merely state capitalism; to an orthodox communist any individualism is bourgeois. If carried to extremes, such attitudes can lead to a breakdown in the cooperation that is required for alliances of the left or the right to survive, and lead to their fragmentation.

Solidarity, on the left or the right, can only come from a toleration of potential allies and their ideological positions. But inevitably issues arise in politics which do not easily lend themselves to left/right distinctions and these can put a heavy strain on such alliances. In British parliamentary terms we know that the liberal legalisation of abortion and homosexuality, the abolition or restoration of the death penalty, have in the past found supporters and opponents in all political parties. Major constitutional issues such as regional autonomy or membership of the EEC have provoked similar divisions. In other words, there are issues which cut across party allegiances and left/right labels, and one group of socialists and conservatives, acting together, will find themselves opposed by an alliance of another group of socialists and conservatives.

It is the contention of this study that there are many welfare issues which do not lend themselves easily to left/right distinctions and that on such issues as control and compulsion it is not always helpful to analyse them in left/right terms. This naturally prompts the question as to whether there is another political spectrum which has a degree of explanatory power where the left/right distinction breaks down. The one which I have found particularly useful is that between a libertarian and an authoritarian perspective.

The distinction is between those who, whatever their attitude towards the ownership of property, believe that the state's role in society should be minimal and those who stress the importance of a strong role for the state. The libertarian emphasis is upon the rights of the individual and on as little state interference as possible.

Libertarians wish to see the state's right to control and compel reduced to an absolute minimum. Individuals should be free to make their own decisions, to determine their own lifestyles, to create their own norms and rules as far as is possible. The authoritarian sees the interests of people as being bound up with the existence of a strong state. Without a strong state there is chaos and indiscipline. Control and compulsion are necessary to the maintenance of social order.

At the extremes we find anarchists on the libertarian left and advocates of *laissez-faire* principles on the libertarian right. On the authoritarian left we would expect to find those sympathetic to Stalinist socialism while on the authoritarian right we would find those sympathetic to fascist and militaristic régimes. It has often been noted that there is some similarity between the language, ideology, principles and practices of the two brands of libertarianism and between the two brands of authoritarianism.

In a less extreme way, there is clearly a great deal of similarity between the language used by conservatives who argue that people must not be allowed to sponge off the state and must be made to stand on their own two feet and the views expressed by the advocates of greater compulsion in the Swedish debate. And it is precisely for this reason that the reformists in Sweden have argued, like Holgersson, that the forces behind the compulsory lobby are reactionary. In order to explain how some individuals and groups on the left show a distinct preference for more authoritarian policies, a circular model is posited which shows that the extremes of left and right meet, and are therefore in a way, identical. Such a view was expressed in an

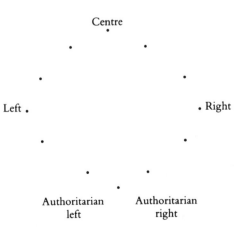

Figure 9.1 The circular model

interview with a senior official of RFHL, and can be represented in the following way.

In this way the authoritarian left can be merged and dismissed along with the other forces of reaction. Admittedly this is merely a schematic representation of a common-sense theory that many people bandy about when they are discussing what they call 'extreme' politics or the similarities between the Stalinist and Nazi states of the 1930s, but it has to be considered if we are to produce a more satisfactory way of explaining the Swedish debate.

However, to combine the far right and left because of an alleged common authoritarianism is highly misleading because, as has already been suggested above, left and right are points on a continuum ranging from a preference for a society in which the means of production are publicly owned to one in which they are privately owned (the inequality axis). In terms of the ownership of the means of production they would be completely different. I would argue instead, that at any point on the left/right continuum we should assume that another cuts diametrically across it, ranging from the authoritarian to the libertarian (the control axis). What this continuum represents is not to do with the ownership of property but with the political organisation of society and the relationship between citizens and the state. A diagrammatic representation would be as follows:

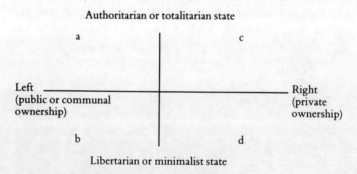

Figure 9.2 The inequality/control matrix

The diagram enables one to place individuals, groups, parties and systems according to their positions on each axis. The stalinist position is represented by (a), the anarchist by (b), the fascist by (c) and the *laissez-faire* by (d). A myriad of positions clustered around the centre would represent the ideologies of social democrats, liberals, corporatists and conservatives. Their location on the matrix would depend upon where they stood upon issues of inequality and control. On issues of inequality, libertarians of the left would share some common ground with authoritarians of the left; on issues of control, libertarians of the left would share some common ground with libertarians of the right, and so on. It clearly follows that alliances of the left or right cut across the authoritarian/libertarian axis and alliances of authoritarians or libertarians cut across the left/right axis.

It is now necessary to show how these distinctions can be applied to the Swedish debate on control. For simplicity's sake, four discrete categories will be used to begin with – the libertarian right, the authoritarian right, the libertarian left and the authoritarian left – before qualifications are made about the nature of the alliances and the extent to which the categories are fixed or enduring.

THE LIBERTARIAN RIGHT

. not represented in debate on drugs (alcohol

The role of the libertarian right was exemplified in the issue on children in care. Family Campaign had a clear anti-socialist and anti-welfare state ideology and wanted to reduce the role of the state in family life. It complained about the excessive supervision of families by welfare professionals which resulted in too many children being taken into care. It accused social workers of using social assistance claims as an excuse for prying into a family's other problems. It complained that psychologists and psychiatrists acted against those it regarded as socially deviant. It accused day nurseries of inculcating young children with marxist ideology. The ultimate cause of these problems was the existence of a strong socialist government, which was determined to make Sweden into a socialist state. Family Campaign argued that the answer to the problem was to cut the welfare state and reduce taxation, in order to restore to parents the possibility of looking after their children on one income, so that they would not have to rely on the state for support.

THE AUTHORITARIAN RIGHT

While the authoritarian right might agree with the members of

Family Campaign about the need for less socialism and less taxation, it would not have accepted a decreased role for the state in the area of social control. Historically, the right has been in favour of a punitive poor law, as we saw in the chapter on the development of Sweden's social services. Moreover the role of the bourgeois government between 1976 and 1982, and bourgeois party representatives on the Commission that proposed a liberalisation of the social services legislation in the 1970s, was markedly un-liberal. Everything was done by the government to water down the reformers' proposals, and the retention of compulsory care for alcoholics and its extension to drug addicts flew in the face of the Commission's recommendations. In the end, the legislation was passed because there had been such overwhelming support for it amongst the various interested parties.

In a 1985 survey of the way that the parties of the Riksdag had voted on 12 issues concerning compulsion in the social services, it was shown that Moderaterna (the conservatives) had voted for more compulsion in all twelve motions; followed by the Centre Party which had voted for seven of them; the Folk party (liberals) three; the Social Democrats two; and VPK (communists) none (ALRO *et al* 1985). Although this shows that the right as a whole was divided, the conservatives were unanimously for more control. They were also in favour of the introduction of mellan-tvång (intermediate force – see Chapter 5). Moreover, all three parties of the right are now in favour of the criminalisation of all non-medicinal use of drugs.

Although RNS has always claimed that its members are drawn from the whole political spectrum, it has also admitted that the party whose drug policy comes closest to its own is that of the conservatives. It is interesting to note that even in 1981, when LVM was being debated in the Riksdag, 55 per cent of the conservative representatives voted against it on the grounds that they wanted a longer period of compulsory care for drug addicts and alcoholics, especially the younger ones. As their spokesperson, Blenda Littmarck, said: 'Experiences from, among others, the Hassela Collective and studies I have recently carried out in the US, show that a total removal from the abuse environment for at least six months to a year can be necessary, especially for the category of young abusers' (Riksdagens Protokoll 15/12/81: p. 100).

It is interesting to note in connection with alliances between the authoritarian right and the authoritarian left, that Hassela is approved by both of them. But we shall come to that in the section after the next.

THE LIBERTARIAN LEFT

Much of the impetus behind the liberalisation of social services legislation and a decreasing reliance upon compulsory measures has come from socialists of one kind or another. The Commission that recommended reform was largely made up of social democrats as was the cooperative committee (see Chapter 3) which shadowed its work. Verdandi is a socialist organisation and RFFR and RFHL members drew much of their support from social democrats and communists. Moreover, many of the social workers and administrators, at all levels of local authority social services departments, as well as the Ministry of Social Affairs and Socialstyrelsen, who have argued and pressed for liberalising reforms have been socialists. They have all argued strongly that the old laws were class-based and victimised the working class, and that a reliance upon control and compulsion was un-socialist. Many of the critics of the Alby social workers and of the Örebro drug policy proposal, were socialists also.

The libertarian left also claims that although the SAP voted for LVM in 1981, it was only as a compromise, to prevent more stringent measures being enacted and that many of those social democrats in the Riksdag who supported mellan-tvång, did so, not out of conviction but out of party loyalty.

THE AUTHORITARIAN LEFT

Be that as it may, it cannot be denied that SAP supported LVM in opposition and has not tried to remove it from the statute books since. The present Minister for Social Affairs, Girtrud Sigurdsen, not only introduced mellan-tvång but would now like to strengthen LVM with a longer period of compulsory care. She must have considerable backing for her policies both within the government and within the party as a whole. It is clear too that she not only lent her support to the Alby social workers but replaced Lars Grönwall, the liberal chairman of the Commission investigating LVU and LVM, and appointed one of the architects of the Örebro drug policy proposal, FMN's Peter Paul Heinemann, as an expert adviser to the Commission. Moreover both Botkyrka Kommun (in which Alby is situated) and Örebro Län are local authorities with socialist majorities. Nor are they unique. Västervik social services, which insists that alcoholics who claim social assistance should be prepared to take anatabus tablets (tablets that cause you to vomit if you drink alcohol) is a social democratic kommun; as is Upplands-Väsby which is regarded by RNS as having a model drugs policy. It is clear that many social democrats favour a controlling and restrictive set of policies for dealing with people with social problems.

Nor is it only amongst social democrats, that we find advocates for such policies. There is a great deal of evidence to associate members of far left sympathies with support for a hard-line welfare policy. Hassela, an institution for young drug addicts, which places a lot of emphasis upon discipline and control, may be supported by those on the authoritarian right, but its credentials are solidly socialist. Ronnby likens the Hassela ideology to that of Soviet behaviourism (see Chapter 8):

> It is assumed that because they have a materialist starting-point, their treatment model is collectivist and thereby radical and progressive, that they have the correct class stand-point and stand in solidarity with the working class ... Hassela makes rather a lot of its 'correct' class stand-point.   (Ronnby 1985: pp. 159 and 160)

Moreover, those associated with Hassela, are often members of RNS also. Nils Bejerot, RNS's major ideologist, helped to found Hassela. His writings are clearly in favour of control policies but they have a distinct left-wing flavour as well: 'If the left does not take in the complexity of the problem and turn away from the abscess, to a lever for a progressive social policy, decay will drift steadily towards chaos and finally fascism' (Bejerot 1978: p. 203). The poison of a commercialised, capitalist society, is ever-present in Bejerot's work. In another example of his writing he says:

> Since the left, in the last year, has begun to see through drug-liberalism and pop-radicalism, I believe that such strong forces will be mobilised against the accelerating social disintegration, that the otherwise inevitable development towards chaos and fascism will be capable of being stopped. Anarchistic-libertarian pop-radicalism must be stopped by the left.   (Bejerot 1978: p. 9)

Not only does Ronnby, as a left libertarian, condemn the authoritarianism of Bejerot and Hassela, but Bejerot equally forcefully condemns the anarchistic drift of permissiveness.

Evidence for the existence of a hard-line authoritarian left influence on welfare policy also came from reformists interviewed, who claimed that many of those on the left who vociferously demanded more control and more compulsion had been members of the now defunct Swedish Communist Party (SKP), an authoritarian party that should not be confused with VPK which has a very liberal record on control issues.

ALLIANCES

It is clear from Chapter 4, that on the children in care issue there was an alliance between the libertarian right and the libertarian left. Both were concerned about the extent to which the social welfare authorities were interfering in the lives of individual families. On the issue of drugs and alcohol, there is also evidence of an alliance between authoritarians of the left and the right. Both would like to see the authorities intervening more strongly. There is also a similarity between the attitudes towards social assistance, held by the supporters of the Alby social workers and conservatives, all of whom would claim that they wanted the poor to stand on their own two feet. But these alliances were themselves confined to particular issues over which the critics felt very strongly that they wanted to bring the maximum pressure to bear on the policies of central government. What is more important is that left and right alliances are even stronger. Those on the right do not have the attachment to the welfare state, full employment and a strong public sector that those on the left share. Family Campaign and its more authoritarian colleagues in the conservative party, are united in their opposition to welfare state expenditure and the high levels of taxation which their members have to pay. Similarly, the libertarian and authoritarian factions of the left, are equally critical of a capitalist society which creates massive social problems, and are united in the view that the resources of society must be distributed more equally in order to give the mass of the population jobs, security and a high standard of living.

THE DYNAMICS OF THE INEQUALITY/CONTROL MATRIX

The framework that the inequality/control matrix has provided has enabled us to categorise some of the participants in the Swedish conflict, but we need also to account for the fact that individuals, pressure groups, political parties and society as a whole may change their positions on the matrix over time and according to different

Conflict and control in welfare policy

circumstances. Some of the evidence presented in the book enables us to speculate a little further as to why such changes may occur.

During the early stages of industrialisation Swedish government was dominated by parties of the right and welfare policy was extremely repressive and controlling. Between 1932 and the early 1970s a succession of social democratic governments established the welfare state and presided over a period of almost continuous economic growth and prosperity in which greater equality was achieved socially, politically and economically. At the same time welfare policy was progressively liberalised culminating in the forces which led to the appointment of the investigating commission into the social services which resulted in the major reforms of 1982. It could be argued that they are the delayed consequence of the radicalism of the 1960s and early 1970s. Even before they had been implemented the political climate had begun to change. The economic crisis that affected international capitalism from the middle of the 1970s, led in many countries, including Sweden, to the election of governments of the right. Even with the return of the social democrats in 1982, it was clear that economic difficulties and constraints would prevent the government implementing any kind of radical programme. The 80s have experienced cutbacks in public and welfare expenditure and a reaction against the trend towards greater equality and liberalisation.

To a certain extent then, we may hypothesise that the politics of inequality and control are similarly influenced by macro-economic changes. But other phenomena have occurred in the last two decades to influence the politics of control which have not followed the same pattern. The prosperity of the 1960s was accompanied by the growth of the drug problem which seems to have reactivated the temperance values, attitudes and policies of the past, while the AIDS disease has awakened fears which have reinforced the demand for controlling measures.

These various socio-economic factors combine to influence the position that society, groups or individuals take on the matrix. One set of events or circumstances may cause a shift to the left or the right, another set, a shift towards more or less control. However the resulting equilibrium should not be seen too deterministically. The movement on the left/right axis bears a similarity to what marxists would call the class struggle. Using that concept others have gone on to describe the state as representing the 'balance of class forces'. The literature on class struggle and the social changes which influence it are extensively documented and need not concern us here. But what literature can illuminate the reasons behind shifts along the control axis? What forces are associated with the tension between those who demand more social and/or state control and those who demand less social and/or state control? A useful starting point might be the writings of that other classical sociologist – Emile Durkheim.

THE COLLECTIVE AND THE INDIVIDUAL

It was one of Durkheim's theses that the whole ethos of individualism in capitalist society was based upon a fundamental misunderstanding of the relationship between the individual and society. It was, he believed, a mistake to suppose that individuals could enjoy freedom without some degree of social regulation and constraint. He agreed that too much constraint was undesirable but claimed that too little left individuals with nothing to guide their behaviour or regulate their aspirations. Too much freedom was more likely to result in increased unhappiness than happiness. Without some moral regulation and constraint people became lost and discontented (Durkheim 1964). But his criticism was not aimed solely at the individualism of capitalism and thinkers such as Spencer. He attacked socialists as well, both the collectivists, who emphasised state control, because the end result would be despotism; and the individualists who wanted the state abolished, because the end result would be anarchy (Durkheim 1899). A modern, complex industrial society, in Durkheim's view, required that a balance be maintained between the power of the state and the rights of individuals, and this could best be done by subordinate and mediating institutions which he referred to as corporations (Gane 1984). This argument applied not only to capitalist societies but to socialist societies as well. Durkheim, as a socialist, criticised those who imagined that such problems would not exist in an ideal communist or anarchist society.

> It is therefore much more important to determine what society is in the process of becoming, what it should and can become in the near future, than to seek to guess at the final and ideal point towards which it is heading. Moreover a pure ideal is unachievable precisely because of those demands made by real life and which it does not take into account.
> (Durkheim 1899)

It follows from Durkheim's argument that in times of severe social malaise there would be a need for a strengthening of the controlling elements within society; in times of stability there would be a relaxation of those controls, depending upon the extent of the malaise and perceptions of that malaise.

It would not be far-fetched to argue that the conflict over Swedish welfare policy that this book has described, has been about a struggle between mediating institutions concerning the extent to which the behaviour of individuals should be regulated and controlled by the authorities. The balance between the opposing forces has shifted over time and according to the state of the economy and the experience and perception of major social problems.

CONCLUSION

It has been the aim of this chapter to argue that to see social control in welfare policy in left/right terms, was to burden that distinction (which should be concerned with matters concerning the distribution of property and economic resources) with phenomena it could not explain. An additional distinction – that between the authoritarian and the libertarian – was suggested, that could more adequately cope with issues of control. The matrix that resulted from a combination of the two axes was used to categorise the various individuals and groups that had taken part in the Swedish conflict and explain the alliances that occurred between them. Finally, it was suggested that some justification for the matrix could be found in the literature generated by Marx's concept of class struggle, and Durkheim's work concerning the moral struggle between society and the individual. Perhaps it may be more fruitful in the future if social theorists, instead of working in one or other of the two traditions, could be persuaded to combine both. The field of social policy would seem to be one which would benefit from such an approach.

CHAPTER TEN

Welfare and control in capitalist society

INTRODUCTION

At the beginning of this book, it was said that the study of the conflict between welfare and control in a country that had not been dominated by governments of the right, might have something to contribute to our understanding of welfare and control in capitalism generally. It was suggested that if state welfare was the result of contradictory forces and served contradictory interests, then, in all probability, the same could be said about control. It is therefore useful to ask not only to what extent are bourgeois interests and conservative goals served by control policies, but also to what extent are working and middle-class interests and socialist goals served by control policies. What this study has shown is that where the provision of welfare has been greatly influenced by socialist aims, it is likely that the controlling aspects of welfare have also been influenced by socialists.

It could be argued that precisely because previous studies have concentrated upon societies with predominantly right-wing governments, they have stressed the repressive nature of social control in welfare policy and have neglected to examine its socialistic aspects. This may also have resulted from the loose way in which the concept of a welfare state has been used.

WELFARE SYSTEMS, STATE WELFARE AND THE WELFARE STATE

The welfare state is a term that is often abused. It is used by a number of writers (for example Wilensky 1976 and Gough 1979) to generalise about the provision of *state welfare* in almost any advanced industrial society, be it capitalist or socialist. It would be more accurate to say that all industrial societies have *welfare systems*. Every industrial society has found it necessary to have the institutional means to provide for the mass education of children; to provide some form of health care for the mass of the population; to organise income maintenance provision for the sick, the old and the unemployed; to cope with social problems and provide housing for some social groups. But this can be and has been done in a variety of ways. As Titmuss and many others have pointed out (Titmuss 1968, Field 1981, Rose 1986) many of these services can be purchased privately or provided by employers, voluntary organisations or trade unions as well as by the state. In Japan there is still a tremendous reliance upon occupational welfare; in the US, upon private welfare; and in the UK, extensive use has always been made of the voluntary sector. The mix, as any student of comparative social policy knows, can vary enormously from one society to another (Rose 1986). The fact that in all these welfare systems we can expect to find some degree of state welfare does not qualify all societies to the title, welfare state. In many of them the provision of state welfare is not only minimal but can be very inegalitarian and positively punitive.

The term 'welfare state' should be applied only to those societies where there is a real commitment to full employment, where health care is provided by the state at a high level for the whole population, free or at minimal charge, where state educational opportunities at all levels are open to all, where those with social problems can expect a whole range of services to provide them with help and support, and where the old, the sick and the unemployed can expect to live at a standard not very different to the one they enjoyed when in employment. These were the aims of the British welfare state when it was set up after the Second World War, although it is open to considerable doubt as to whether the term still applies to this country. It was the aim and remains the aim of the Scandinavian countries and, in particular, of Sweden. It must not be forgotten that many of those individuals and groups who have been referred to in previous chapters, as being in favour of more stringent controls in the provision of welfare, would also strongly argue for the maintenance and advancement of the ideals upon which the welfare state is based.

To those critics of the Swedish welfare state, who compare its deficiencies with their utopian visions of a perfect free market, a classless society or a communal paradise, it may be suggested that a

174

more appropriate comparison might be with those existing industrial societies that have failed to achieve the high standard of living and high degree of security enjoyed by the mass of the Swedish population.

There does seem to be an enormous difference between social control in a capitalist society in which state welfare is at a minimum and one where the existence of a welfare state reduces social problems and the need for dependence upon social assistance. There are many examples of the former, where unemployment is allowed to run rife, social insurance benefits are inadequate and rights to them restricted, and where the costs of decent housing are prohibitive. In such societies a class of social assistance dependants is created which social workers and social assistance officials are too hard-pressed to deal with properly. Excessive control mechanisms become administratively necessary and repressive in nature. The very creation of a mass of welfare dependants can be used by powerful groups to control and punish them and excite the hostility of the rest of the population towards them.

Nowhere is this more true than in the US. Merriam complained in the 1960s that the authorities in the US refused to raise social insurance benefits even though this would clearly reduce the need for people to claim social assistance (Jenkins 1969: p. 76). Titmuss described the social assistance system in America as one which stimulated fraud, encouraged dependency and was administered arbitrarily and restrictively. He went on to quote the *Report of the National Advisory Commission on Civil Disorders* which in 1968 concluded that 'Our present system of public welfare is designed to save money instead of people and tragically ends up doing neither' (Ibid.: p. 153). Furniss and Tilton, comparing the US with Britain and Sweden in the mid-70s, claimed that there was simply no concerted effort in America to provide security for the 'large numbers of casualties of the industrial order', and insisted that its failure to provide full employment or comprehensive health care disqualified it from being ranked alongside what were, at that time, the welfare states of Britain and Europe (Furniss and Tilton 1977: p. 182).

This same story is repeated a decade on, in Patterson's historical account of poverty and income maintenance programmes in the US in the twentieth century. He claimed that despite some major achievements in the late 60s and early 70s, 36 million Americans lived in poverty at the beginning of the 80s, and that the attempt to bring about a long overdue, thorough going reform of welfare policy, failed to get through the US legislature in 1980. Moreover, during the next two years the Reagan administration had set about dismantling the modest reforms of the previous fifteen years – one billion dollars was saved and 700,000 people lost some or all of their benefits (Patterson 1986: p. 212).

Similar changes in the governments of Margaret Thatcher have disqualified Britain's claim to be a welfare state. The ease with which this has been accomplished would not surprise those outside commentators, who in various studies over the years, have found the British system lacking in comparison with its European counterparts. Heclo, in his examination of the development of social policy, showed that Sweden's experience of poor law deterrence had been nothing like as harsh as Britain's (Heclo 1974: p. 17). Ashford argued that the British had never managed to implement a systematic, social democratic, corporatist vision of welfare linked with a wages policy, in the way that France, West Germany and Sweden had. The Beveridge reforms of the 1940s had for many years concealed the essentially ambiguous attitudes of the British to the idea of a welfare state (Ashford 1986). Britain's income maintenance system is regarded by Heidenheimer as pragmatic compared with the coherent and positive programmes of Sweden and West Germany (Heidenheimer *et al.* 1983: p. 217). It is hardly surprising, in this context, that Conservative governments have been able to preside over record levels of unemployment, the growth of social assistance claimants, reductions in social insurance entitlements and a weakening of state health care and education services. The increasing control in such a system has to be seen against a background of a weakening commitment to the concept of a welfare state.

In the Swedish welfare state, where full employment is regarded as a priority, where pensioners and the sick have a right to a high level of benefit, where people of all classes can be decently housed, the reliance upon social assistance is kept to a minimum. In such a society controlling measures may be harsh – they may sometimes be unnecessary or even counter-productive – but they cannot be simply dismissed as examples of capitalist repression. They may, on the contrary, be examples of how best to avoid it.

SOCIALISM, SOCIAL ASSISTANCE AND SOCIAL CONTROL

Socialists in Sweden have been united in their defence of the welfare state. What divides them, according to this study, is the extent to which citizens with social problems and who need social assistance, should be made to help themselves. Some have argued that such people are the victims of a capitalist society and should have considerable help and support to enable them to achieve independence and fulfilment. Others have argued that such people often need more than help and encouragement. As they see it they would be failing in their duty as socialists, if they allowed fellow workers to slide further down the road to destitution, dependence and addiction. People may *have* to be *persuaded* or *made* to have help.

Moreover some of those who have problems and claim social assistance may be seen not as fellow workers but as members of the reactionary lumpenproletariat. Such a view was expressed by Jan Myrdal at an RNS meeting in 1977.

> The proletariat and the lumpenproletariat do not belong to the same class. The lumpenproletariat is a product of capitalism and is recruited from all the different layers of society but chiefly from the working class and those thrown out of the petite bourgeoisie. The whole of this floating stratum of thieves, ponces, drug-suppliers, fences and prostitutes and so forth, have in common that they neither carry out nor seek to carry out any kind of socially useful work. There is a great difference between the lumpenproletariat and sick and unemployed workers. (Lind and Hartelius 1982: p. 31)

From the point of view of a socialist like Myrdal, laws and policies which control the lumpenproletariat not only benefit the working class but are widely supported by them.

Similar sentiments have been embodied in the welfare policies of countries like the USSR and China. In the decades after the 1917 revolution, welfare rights and the right to work were not unconditional: 'It is certainly not accidental that a constitution that guarantees the worker's maintenance and the right to work, also imposes on him the duty to work' (Rimlinger 1971: p. 256).

Although the more severe measures that were used to deal with absenteeism, lateness, loafing and drunkenness in the 1930s, have been replaced by an emphasis upon welfare objectives, Rimlinger insists that social welfare in the Soviet Union, in the years following the death of Stalin, remained 'a means of social control through the involvement of the masses in the activities of the state' (Ibid.: p. 293).

Dixon has argued that Chinese socialism has emphasised the values of diligence, frugality, thrift and the work ethic and that as a result, the welfare system reinforces these values 'by providing only minimal relief to its recipients, based largely on their individual needs' (Dixon 1981: p. 14). Measures are taken to ensure that those

177

capable of supporting themselves and their families should not be eligible for social assistance (Ibid.).

It is not surprising therefore to discover that Swedish socialists may differ about who should or should not be entitled to social assistance. The distinction between the deserving and the undeserving remains a dilemma even in the most generous welfare system. The distinction may be made with more or less severity, with lesser or harsher conditions attached, but it still has to be made. It is a distinction made not just by the 'ruling class' but by middle and working-class people too. Socialists may not want to exaggerate the distinction but they would be foolish to ignore it. In Sweden socialists do everything to ensure that people do not need to claim social assistance but they still argue about what controls and demands should be placed upon those that do.

Might not the success and power of the Swedish labour movement be partly the result of this ability to balance the twin demands for welfare and control? Might the continuing support of the working class for the social democrats and their welfare state be precisely because, on the one hand, it provides security for all, but, on the other, insists that if people will not or cannot help themselves, the authorities will encourage or force them to do so?

NEGLECT AND INTERFERENCE IN SOCIAL WORK

The dilemmas faced by Swedes in the administration of social welfare are universal ones. There will always be cases where the decision about whether or not to intervene in people's social problems is not clear cut. In such circumstances there will be individual social workers who will make the 'wrong' decision and, justifiably or not, be accused either of undue interference or irresponsible neglect. Recent media discussions of such cases in the UK have tended to stress the responsibility or otherwise of individual workers,[1] but these matters are also a question of resources, policies and decisions at higher levels – the social services department, the local authority or central government. Attempts by the authorities to find the 'correct' balance, to escape the accusation of neglect or interference will never be entirely successful. The conflicts in Sweden about social welfare legislation, the role of Socialstyrelsen, local authorities and the social work profession, show that, in spite of the welfare state, the dilemmas do not disappear. A degree of neglect is the inevitable consequence of the voluntary approach while a degree of interference is bound to follow an emphasis upon compulsion.

What this study has tried to illustrate is the way in which the participants in the Swedish debates have mobilised their arguments and forces. On the one hand it has been shown that the conflict has been a very structured one, both historically and in the present. On the other hand that structure has not been of a kind predicted by much of the academic literature on social control.

CONCLUSION

If too monolithic a view is taken of the concept of social control then 'society', 'capitalism', 'the ruling class', or 'welfare bureaucrats and professionals' come to be seen as totally controlling. While such perspectives are a useful corrective to a naive, humanitarian approach to the study of social policy, they can be misleading and one-sided. Within the welfare system of one capitalist country, we have seen how social control can be championed by forces on the left and the right of politics, by some social workers and local authorities and not others, by different individuals and groups, who attach different meanings and motivations to their actions. Part of the Swedish debate about control concerns attitudes towards the poor and those who abuse social assistance; part is about attitudes towards those who have become dependent on drugs or alcohol to the extent that they are perceived as being a threat to themselves and others around them; part is about the extent to which the state should intervene in people's private lives to help people help themselves. It would seen reasonable to suggest that while some features of this debate may be peculiar to Sweden, these conclusions probably apply to all industrial societies. If social welfare itself can be seen as the product of a number of competing goals and aspirations, so can social control.

NOTE

1. I am thinking particularly of the cases of Kimberley Carlile (see the report in the *Guardian* 12 December 1987) and Tyra Henry (see the report in the *Guardian* 19 December 1987) where social workers were accused of

neglect which resulted in the two children being beaten to death, and the investigation into the large numbers of children taken into care by Cleveland Social Services (extensively reported in the British press throughout 1987) where doctors and social workers were accused of unnecessary interference.

Glossary

SWEDISH TERMS

Kommun
  Municipality
Kommunförbundet (see Svenska Kommunförbundet)
Län
  County
Länstyrelse
  County Administrative Board
Socialdepartementet
  The Ministry for Health and Social Affairs
Socialstyrelsen
  The National Board for Health and Social Welfare (In Sweden,
  small central government ministries appoint semi-independent
  boards to carry out day to day administration)
Svenska Kommunförbundet
  The Swedish Association of Municipal Councils

Abbreviations

AMS – Arbetsförmedlingen
  Local employment services agency
FK – Familjekampanjen
  Family campaign, a pressure group
FMN – Föräldrar mot narkotika
  Parents against drugs, a pressure group
JK – Juridisk Kansler
  Judicial Chancellor

181

Conflict and control in welfare policy

LO - Landsorganisation
Confederation of manual worker trade unions
LTU - Lag om tvångsomhändertagande av unga
The proposal for a new law on the compulsory care of the young
LVM - Lag om vård av missbrukare
The law on the care of alcoholics and drug-abusers (1982)
LVU - Lag om vård av unga
The law on the care of young people (1982)
RFFR - Riksförbundet för familjers rättigheter
National association for family rights
RFHL - Riksförbundet för hjälp åt läkemedelsmissbrukare
National association to help addicts
RNS - Riksförbundet Narkotikafritt Samhälle
National association for a drug-free society
SAP - Socialdemokratiska Arbetareparti
The social democratic workers party
SB - Socialbidrag
Means-tested social assistance
SEK
Swedish Kronor
SOFT - Socialförsäkringstillägg
A scheme whereby much SB would be administered by the social
insurance authorities
SoL - Socialtjänstlagen
Social services law (1982)
SSM - Samarbetskommittén för socialvårdens målfrågor
Cooperative committee for social care questions
TCO - Tjänstemännens Centralorganisation
Confederation of white collar trade unions
VPK - Vänsterpartiet Kommunisterna
The communist party

Bibliography

ALRO and Verdandi 1985 'Viktigt meddelande inför valet'; Leaflet published by Alro and Verdandi

Anderson, D., Lait, J. and Marsland, D. 1981 *Breaking the spell of the welfare state:* The Social Affairs Unit

Ashford, D. E. 1986 *The emergence of the welfare states,* Basil Blackwell

Bager-Sjögren, U. 1984 *LVU en uppföljningsundersökning,* Stockholms Universitet-Socialhögskolan

Bejerot, N. 1978 *Missbruk av alkohol, narkotika och frihet,* Ordfront Botyrka Kommun 1985 *Alby: Yttrande till Socialstyrelsen,* 20 May

Boucher, L. 1982 *Tradition and change in Swedish education,* Pergamon

Brown, A. 1981 'Sweden: abuse of children' *The Spectator,* 3 October

Brown, A. 1983 'Ill fares the biggest welfare state' *The Times,* 27 May

Brown, A. 1984 'Swedish motherhood' *The Spectator,* 2 June

Butt-Philip, A. 1978 *Creating New Jobs,* Policy Studies Institute

CAN 1982 *Alcohol policy in Sweden,* Stockholm

CAN 1985 *Rapport,* Stockholm

Castles, F. and McKinlay, R. 1979 'The sheer futility of the sociological approach to politics' *British Journal of Political Science,* vol. 19

Castles, F. 1978 *The social democratic image of society,* Routledge and Kegan Paul

Cohen, S. and Scull, A. (eds) 1985 *Social control and the state,* Basil Blackwell

Corrigan, P. and Leonard, P. 1978 *Social work practice under capitalism,* Macmillan

Criminal Statistics for England and Wales 1982 *Cmnd 9048,* HMSO

Daily Mail 1981 *The state that snatches children,* 2 May

183

Conflict and control in welfare policy

Davies, P. and Walsh, D. 1983 *Alcohol problems and alcohol control in Europe*, Croom Helm

DHSS 1985 *Mental health statistics for England. Booklet two: mental illness and mental handicap*

Dixon, J. 1981 *The Chinese welfare system*, Praeger

Durkheim, É. 1899 'Review of Merlinos's *Formes et essences du socialisme' economy and society*, vol. 13, no. 3, 1984

Durkheim, É. 1964 *The division of labour in society*, The Free Press, New York

Economist 1981 *Swedish industry's thin upper crust*, 4 April

Economist 1987 *The non-conformist state*, 7 March

Elmér Å 1948 *Svensk socialpolitik*, Gleerups, Malmö

Elmér Å 1983 *Svensk socialpolitik*, Liber Förlag, Malmö

Expressen 1986a 'Så myglades Barbro Westerholm bort' 6 April

Expressen 1986b 'Skräckväldet blev föredöme' 8 April

Field, F. 1981 *Inequality in Britain*, Fontana

Financial Times 1986 'Sweden', 25 January

FMN 1985 *Drogpolitiskt program*, Malmö

Fornell, L. 1985 'Värst är det "fina" förtrycket i Alby', *Socionomen* Nr 17

Furniss, N. and Tilton, T. 1977 *The case for the welfare state*, Indiana University Press

Gane, M. 1984 'Institutional socialism and the sociological critique of communism, *Economy and society*, vol. 13, no. 3

Golding, P. and Middleton, S. 1982 *Images of welfare*, Martin Robertson

Gough, I. 1979 *The political economy of the welfare state*, Macmillan

Gould, A. 1984a 'Sweden: still streets ahead', *Social work today*, 27 February

Gould, A. 1984b 'Swedish educational leave in practice', *Discussion Paper no. 12*, Association for Recurrent Education

Greve, J. 1978 *Low incomes in Sweden*, Background paper to Report No. 6 Royal Commission on the distribution of incomes and wealth, HMSO

Grönwall, L. and Nasenius, J. 1982 *Socialtjänstens mål och medel*, Skeab

Grosin, L. 1985 'En solidaritetsyn med rötter i arbetarrörelsen' *Socionomen*, Nr 28

Hale, J. 1983 'Scandinavian journey', BBC Radio Four, 10 August

Handler, J. F. 1973 *The coercive social worker*, Rand McNally

Heclo, H. 1974 *Modern social politics*, Yale University Press

Heidenheimer, A. J., Heclo, H. and Adams, C. T. 1983 *Comparative public policy*, Macmillan

Heidenheimer, A. J. and Elander, N. 1980 *The shaping of the Swedish health system*, St Martins
Hempel, T. 1985 'Voters to the Riksdag' *Current Sweden* No. 341, The Swedish Institute
Hessle, S. 1982 'Socialarbeterna och omhändertagandeproblematiken' *Socionomen*, No 25
Higgins, J. 1978 *The poverty business*, Basil Blackwell
Higgins, J. 1980 'Social control theories of social policy' *Journal of social policy*, vol 9, pt 1
Holden, A. 1980 *Children in care*, Comyn Books
Holgersson, L. 1981 *Socialvård*, Tidens
Holgersson, L. 1986 'Nio skäl att ej straffbelägga bruket av narkotika' *Socialt Arbete*, Nr 8
Hollander, A. 1985 *Omhändertagande av barn*, Aktuell Juridik
Hollander, A. 1986 *LVU blir LTU SSR*, Tidningen No 28
Illich, I. 1971 *De-schooling society*, Calder and Boyars
Illich, I. 1976 *Limits to medicine*, Boyars
Illich, I. 1977 *Disabling professions*, Boyars
International Labour Office 1979 *The cost of social security 1972-74*
International Labour Office 1981 *The cost of social security 1975-77*
International Labour Office 1985 *The cost of social security 1978-80*
Jenkins, S. (ed.) 1969 *Social security in international perspective*, Columbia University Press
Johansson, S. 1980 *Barnens välfärd*, Institutet för Social Forskning, Stockholm University
Jones, C. 1983 *The state, social work and the working class*, Macmillan
Jones, W. 'Swedish adult education observed' *Adult education*, vol. 49, May 1976
Jordan, B. 1981 *Automatic poverty*, Routledge and Kegan Paul
Karlskoga 1986 *Remiss: Narkotikapolitiskt program för Örebro Län*, Socialtjänsten i Karlskoga
Karlskoga Kommun 1985 'Statistik'
Karlskoga Kommun 1986 'Budget 1986'
Karlskoga Kuriren 1986 'Hembränt en utländsk import' 5 May
Kemeny, J. 1981a *Swedish rental housing*, Centre for Urban and Regional Studies, University of Birmingham
Kemeny, J. 1981b *The myth of home ownership*, Routledge and Kegan Paul
Kincaid, J. C. 1975 *Poverty and equality in Britain*, Penguin
Kristensson, P. and Landahl, E. 1985 'Förnedrande arbetssätt i Alby?' *Socionomen*, Nr 14

Conflict and control in welfare policy

Länsstyrelsen 1986 *Uppföljning av förhållandena vid Alby kontoret, 10 April*

Larsson, S. and Sjöström, K. 1979 'The welfare state myth in class society' in Fry. J. *The limits of the welfare state*, Saxon House

Leivonhufvud, S. 1982 'New departures from the middle road' *Current Sweden* No 295, The Swedish Institute

Lind, J. and Hartelius, J. 1982 *Kamp mot knarket*, P. A. Norstedt, Stockholm

Lindblom, P. 1982 *Socialpolitiken*, Almqvist and Wiksell, Stockholm

Lindgren, S. 1987 'Bredda huvudspåret', *Slå Tillbaka*, Nr 1-2, RFHL, Stockholm

Linton, M. 1984 'By all accounts they should be bust', *The Guardian* 9 October

Linton, M. 1985 *The Swedish road to socialism*, Fabian Society

Löfholm, B. 1985 *Inledningsanförande vid debatt om ansvarsmodellen* (Typescript of an unpublished speech)

Lundqvist, S. 1975 'Popular movements and reforms 1900–1920 in Koblik 8, *Sweden's development from poverty to affluence 1750–1970*, University of Minnesota Press, Minneapolis

Mattson, H. 1984 *Den goda förmyndaren*, Liber, Stockholm

Ministry of Health and Social Affairs 1981 *Social services act*, Stockholm

Ministry of Health and Social Affairs 1982 *Care of alcoholics and drug-abusers*, Stockholm

Ministry of Health and Social Affairs 1983 *Information memorandum no. 3*, Stockholm

Mishra, R. 1984 *The welfare state in crisis*, Wheatsheaf

Mörner, C. 1985 'Jag känner mig fasa över Socialstyrelsens Agerande i Alby' *Socionomen*, Nr 20

Mosey, C. 1983 'Karl and Goliath grips Sweden' *Observer*, 30 October

Mosey, C. 1984 'Spectre of children's gulag haunts Sweden' *Observer*, 19 August

Myrbäck, S. 1986 'RNS-Kongressen' *Narkotikafrågan*, Nr 35 RNS, Stockholm

Myrbäck, S. 1987 'På rymmen från LVM' *Narkotikafrågan*, Nr 39, RNS, Stockholm

National Swedish Council for Crime Prevention 1984, *Current Swedish Legislation on Narcotics*

Narkotikafrågan 1985 'Fult regeringen' Nr 30, RNS, Stockholm

Narkotikafrågan 1985 'Mellan-tvång införs igen', Nr 31, RNS, Stockholm

Narkotikafrågan 1986 'JK friar Socialstyrelsen', Nr 34, RNS,

Stockholm
Nilsson, I. 1985 'Smittskyddslagen ändras' *Slå Tillbaka*, Nr 5, RFHL, Stockholm
Nilsson, M. 1985 'Värst i Europa', *Slå Tillbaka*, Nr 5, RFHL, Stockholm
Nordisk Ministerråd 1985 *Barnevern i Norden*, Oslo
Novak, T. 1984 *Poverty and social security*, Pluto Press
ÖKR 1985 Från Dårhus till sjukhus, ÖKR Tidskrift vol 15 No 6
Organisation for Economic Cooperation and Development 1984 *National accounts*
Örebro 1984 *Kommundelsfakta*
Örebro Län 1984 *Narkotikapolitiskt program för Örebro Län*
Örebro Län 1986 *Narkotikapolitiskt program för Örebro Län*
Packman, J., Randall, J. and Jacques, N. 1986 *Who needs care?* Basil Blackwell
Partistyrelsens Förslag 1987 'Ett samhälle där vi bryr oss om varandra', *Socialdemokraterna*
Patterson, J. T. 1986 *America's struggle against poverty 1900–1985*, Harvard University Press
Persson, M. 1985b 'Personalen i Alby', *Socionomen*, Nr 15
Persson, B. 1987 'Sant och falskt om LTU', *Socionomen*, Nr 3
Philip, A. B. 1978 *Creating new jobs*, Policy Studies Institute
Piven, F. F. and Cloward R. A. 1972 *Regulating the poor*, Tavistock
RFFR 1983 *Missbruk omhändertaganden misstag*, R-Pocket, Stockholm
RFHL 1985 *Princip och handlingsprogram*, Stockholm
Riksdagen 1985 *Votering SOU 31*, 31 May
Riksdagens Protokoll 1981 *LVM*, 15 December
Rimlinger, G. V. 1971 *Welfare policy and industrialisation in Europe, America and Russia*, John Wiley
Ronnby, A. 1985 *Socialstaten* Studentlitteratur, Lund
Rose, R. 1986 *The welfare state: east and west*, Oxford University Press
Rydelius, P.-A. 1981 *Barn till alkoholiserade fäder*, Liber, Stockholm
Scase, R. 1977 *Social democracy in capitalist society*, Croom Helm
Shenfield, A. 1980 *The failure of socialism*, The Heritage Foundation, Washington DC
Sjöstedt, J. 1985 'Knarkjakten', *Socialt arbete*, Nr 10
Sjöström, K. 1984 *Social Politiken*, Arbetarkultur, Stockholm
Slå Tillbaka 1985 'AIDS kan skapa våldsam hysteri', Nr 5, RFHL, Stockholm
Socialdepartementet 1986:7 *Socialbidrag – Delrapport från en arbetsgrupp*

Conflict and control in welfare policy

Socialstyrelsen 1981 *Rätter till bistånd*
Socialstyrelsen 1985 *En vanlig människa*, Stockholm
Socialstyrelsen 1985a *Alby: Tillsynspromenoria*, 13 March
Socialstyreslen 1985b *Alby: Ytterligare material* 19 April
Socialstyrelsen 1985c *Alby: Beslut i tillsynsärende* 2 July
Socionomen 1985 'Alby – toppen av ett isberg', Nr 14
SOU 1979/80:44 *Socialutskottets betänkande*, Stockholm
SOU 1984:64 *Psykiatrin, tvånget och rättssäkerheten*, Stockholm
SOU 1986:20 *Barns behov och föräldrars rätt*, Stockholm
SOU 1986:21 *Barns behov och föräldrars rätt (sammanfattning)*,
   Stockholm
Statistisk Årsbok 1986 Statistiska Centralbyrån
Stenberg, S. 1985 'Socialstyrelsens promenoria om Alby var som gjord
   för en enkel journalistik', *Socionomen*, Nr 22
Sundelin, A. 1985 *Det märkliga spelet kring Alby*, Narkotikafrågan,
   Nr 32, RNS, Stockholm
Sunesson, S. 1985 *Ändra Allt*, Liber, Malmö
Svensk Författnings-Samling 1903 P. A. Norstedt, Stockholm
Svensk Författnings-Samling 1919 P. A. Norstedt, Stockholm
Svenska Kommunförbundet 1984 *Socialtjänstens insatser för
   ungdomar* 25 January
Svenska Kommunförbundet 1985a *Samtal om samarbetsklimatet
   mellan samarbetspartner och socialbyrån i Alby*
Svenska Kommunförbundet 1985b *Alby: Klientberättelser*, 24 April
Swedish Institute 1985 *Alcohol and drug abuse in Sweden*, Fact sheet,
   Stockholm
Titmuss, R. M. 1958 *Essays on the welfare state*, Allen and Unwin
Tomasson, R. F. 1970 *Sweden: prototype of modern society*, Random
   House, New York
UNESCO 1977 *Statistical yearbook 1977*
UNESCO 1983 *Statistical yearbook 1982*
Usher, R. 1979 'University reform and adult education in Sweden'
   Studies in Adult Education, vol 11, No 1
Verdandi 1985 *Handling är det bästa politiska språket*, Stockholm
Wicks, M. 1987 'Mr Moore's welfare stakes' *New Statesman*, 5 October
Wilensky, H. L. 1975 *The welfare state and equality*, University of
   California Press
Wilson, D. 1979 *The welfare state in Sweden*, Heinemann
Worsthorne, P. 1978 'Too much freedom', in Cowling, M. *Con-
   servative essays*, Cassell
Worsthorne, P. 1983 'The poor as pawns in the political game', *Daily
   Telegraph*, 28 August

Index

statistics on, 56–64, 68
voluntary, 56, 58, 61
institutional, 38–9, 47
of the elderly, 38–9, 47
of the mentally ill, 75
open, 47
Carlsson, I. 128
Centre Party, (see also, bourgeois
government, bourgeois parties),
29–30, 46, 166
central government, 29–31, 169
Central Organisation for Social Work,
36–7
China
socialism, 177
welfare policies in, 177–8
class
interests, 151, 158
laws, 41, 121, 148
middle class, 150
ruling class, 6, 151–2, 179
struggle, 170–2
underclass, 72–3
working class, 6, 50, 71, 149, 151, 178
Cohen, S. and Scull, A. 9–10
Commission, the, 42, 48, 70, 72, 96–7,
128, 146, 150, 170
composition of, 48, 167
proposals, 44, 49, 93, 166
reports, 43, 70–3, 75, 140
Communist Party (VPK), 30, 97, 135,
166, 169
the Swedish (SKP), 134, 168
comparative perspective, 14, 24–9
consensus, 5
theories, 4, 12
Conservative Party, (see also, bourgeois
government, bourgeois parties),
29–30, 133–4, 166, 169
contact persons and contact families, 60,
98, 141
clients of, 85–6, 90–6
costs of, 85
differences between contact persons
and contact families, 85
duties of, 80–2, 84–85
origins of, 80–2
payment of, 82
controlling function, 82, 87–90, 92
survey of, 78, 82–96
control, 145, 148, 152, 154, 175–6, 179
conflict between welfare and, 4, 53,
95–6, 172–3, 178
in welfare policies, 3–16, 31, 45, 49,
95–7, 150–151, 159–61, 170, 172,
175

theories of, 4–10, 12
Cooperative Committee for Social
Welfare
Questions, 43, 146, 167
corporatism, 27
CSA, (see Central Organisation for
Social Work)

Denmark
AIDS and compulsion, 140
children in care, 55, 63–4
compulsory care of the mentally ill,
75
divorce, 64, 69, 156
drugs
abuse and addiction, 41, 44–5, 69, 73,
75, 86, 98, 100, 105, 113, 118,
119–42, 134, 156, 169–70, 179
compulsory care, 38, 43, 46–9, 126–7,
138, 140–1, 142n, 166
compulsory care, numbers in, 126
extent of problem, 123
indicators of, 73–4
legislation concerning, 46–9, 120,
125–6, 138–41, 142n, 146, 148, 167
police and, 123
urine tests for, 136–7
voluntary treatment for, 47, 126
Durkheim, É. 171–2

education, 23
expenditure, 25
elections, 29–30, 48

Family campaign, 65–6, 165–6, 169
Family rights association (see National
association for family rights)
Finland
children in care, 55, 63–4
FMN (see Parents against drugs)
Folkpartiet (see Liberal Party)
Föräldrar Mot Narkotika (see Parents
against drugs)
France, 25, 122, 176
free church movement, 18, 121
free market economy, 155–8
full employment, 31–2, 40, 157, 176
functionalism, 4, 9, 14

Gough, I. 6, 10
Grönwall, L. 37–40, 167
Grosin, L. 114

Handler, J. F. 5–6
Hassela, 134, 154, 166, 168
health care, 22, 26